Animal Planet™

American Pit Bull Terriers

ELAINE WALDORF GEWIRTZ

American Pit Bull Terriers

Project Team
Editor: Stephanie Fornino
Copy Editor: Ellen Bingham
Interior Design: Leah Lococo Ltd. and Stephanie Krautheim
Design Layout: Tilly Grassa

T.F.H. Publications
President/CEO: Glen S. Axelrod
Executive Vice President: Mark E. Johnson
Publisher: Christopher T. Reggio
Production Manager: Kathy Bontz

T.F.H. Publications, Inc.
One TFH Plaza
Third and Union Avenues
Neptune City, NJ 07753

Discovery Communications, Inc. Book Development Team
Maureen Smith, Executive Vice President & General
 Manager, Animal Planet
Carol LeBlanc, Vice President, Marketing and Retail
 Development
Elizabeth Bakacs, Vice President, Creative Services
Peggy Ang, Director, Animal Planet Marketing
Caitlin Erb, Marketing Associate

Printed and bound in China

07 08 09 10   3 5 7 9 8 6 4 2
ISBN13 9-780793-837588
Library of Congress Cataloging-in-Publication Data

Gewirtz, Elaine Waldorf.
  American pit bull terriers / Elaine Waldorf Gewirtz.
    p. cm. — (Animal Planet pet care library)
  Includes index.
  ISBN 0-7938-3758-8 (alk. paper)
  1. American pit bull terrier. I. Animal Planet (Television network) II. Title. III. Series.
  SF429.A72G49 2006
  636.755'9—dc22

The Leader In Responsible Animal Care For Over 50 Years!™

www.tfh.com

Table of Contents

Chapter 1

Why I Adore My
APBT

To know the American Pit Bull Terrier (APBT) is to love him, despite his often negative portrayal by the media. Courageous yet sensitive, outgoing but devoted, this breed causes a buzz wherever he goes. Everyone has an opinion about APBTs, but are they devils or are they angels? After a number of dog attacks, some people believe that APBTs are too aggressive for their own good and should be banned.

everal cities in the United States and a few European countries have proposed legislation prohibiting the breed, but APBT owners believe that the breed's loyalty, intelligence, and sense of humor have a strong place in American history that's hard to deny. For example, Stubby, an American Pit Bull Terrier from Connecticut, earned the rank of sergeant and was a celebrated hero of World War I, having captured a German spy on the battlefield. During the Civil War, a brindle APBT named Sallie refused to leave wounded men in her regiment at Gettysburg.

During the first half of the last century, APBTs were the most popular breed in America. More than just a pretty face, APBTs today work as drug- and bomb-sniffing dogs with U.S. Customs officials, and thousands of APBTs visit nursing homes, hospitals, and schools each year as certified therapy dogs.

All living things have the potential to do good and evil. With the strength and character APBTs have, they are ready, willing, and able to follow whatever

The APBT's loyalty, intelligence, and sense of humor are legendary.

direction their owners choose for them. It is the individual APBT and his owner, rather than the breed as a whole, who should be judged. The future of the American Pit Bull Terrier rests in the hands of responsible dog owners.

Physical Characteristics

All breeds look the way they do for a reason. In fact, over the course of many generations, breeders sculpted their breeds by selecting physical traits that helped their dogs perform specific tasks.

Origin of the APBT's Physical Makeup

If you observe the athletic build of an APBT, you will be able to understand his heritage. APBTs were originally used by butchers to manage bulls and by hunters to help catch and hold wild boar and other game. In England, these tasks evolved to become the sport of bull baiting, the act of pitting dogs against bulls or bears, until it was outlawed in 1835. Dog fighting sprang up in its place and preserved a role for a dog who possessed sheer strength, stamina, and the biting and wrestling ability to take on another animal to its death. Although dog fighting is illegal today, some communities in the United States still secretly stage one dog against another in a pit (hence the origin of the APBT's name), but the majority of modern-day APBTs do not participate in this reprehensible activity.

What remains of the APBT's heritage is his appearance. To maintain this vision as a stalwart fighting breed, breeders composed a written description, called a *breed standard,* of what the breed should look and act like. To prove the dog's merit, many APBT owners advocate testing with weight-pulling competitions rather than fighting, because the physical requirements of both activities are similar.

Today, the same dog can be registered as an American Pit Bull

Famous APBT Owners

As more people learn how wonderful this breed is, the list of famous APBT owners continues to grow: Fred Astaire, Linda Blair, Vin Diesel, rapper DMX a.k.a. Earl Simmons, Thomas Edison, Ken Howard, Steve Irwin, Stephan Jenkins, Helen Keller, Frankie Muniz, Judd Nelson, Rosie Perez, Bernadette Peters, Theodore Roosevelt, Julian Schnabel, Alicia Silverstone, Sinbad, John Steinbeck, John Stewart, Mark Twain, Usher, Laura Ingalls Wilder, and Woodrow Wilson all own or owned APBTs. Broadway dog trainer Bill Berloni has trained a total of six American Pit Bull Terriers for Broadway and off-Broadway shows.

Terrier in the United Kennel Club (UKC) and the American Dog Breeders Association (ADBA). A similar-looking dog, called the American Staffordshire Terrier (or Am Staff), can be registered with the American Kennel Club (AKC). Why the difference?

The APBT was originally used in dog fighting, a popular sport in the

The Expert Knows

A Dog With a Job

The APBT has distinguished itself as a versatile working dog, capable of being a search-and-rescue dog. Using their superior intelligence, APBTs easily learn tracking and air-scenting rescue techniques. They also perform vital duties as drug- and bomb-detection dogs. Loyal and strong, APBTs aren't afraid of danger and put people's safety ahead of their own.

breed's association with fighting prevented it from gaining AKC recognition. However, by identifying the breed as a Staffordshire Terrier, it became eligible for AKC registration in 1936. The name changed to American Staffordshire Terrier in 1972 to differentiate it from the Staffordshire Terrier of England. Originally descended from British Bulldogs and English Terriers, the APBT and the Am Staff have been bred independently for more than 60 years.

United States during the 1800s. Breeders selectively bred the strongest, most aggressive dogs for fighting but rejected dogs who snapped or attacked their handlers. When owners wanted to show their APBTs in AKC competition, the

What the Modern-Day APBT Looks Like

In conformation competition (dog showing), the judges evaluate how closely a dog comes to the written standard. Although the UKC and ADBA have different standards for this breed, the overall reason that the

dog was originally bred is the same.

The ADBA standard uses a 100-point description that relates mostly to evaluating fighting ability, while the UKC mentions personality and obedience. The standards are alike in that most APBTs are between 18 inches (45.7 cm) and 22 inches (55.9 cm) tall when measured at the shoulders. The dog's weight should range from 30 pounds (13.6 kg) to 80 pounds (36.3 kg). In terms of height and weight, most males are larger and heavier than most females.

This is a breed in which the block-like shape of the head is very important. It should be wide between the ears and eyes and have flat cheeks. The muzzle should be medium in length and the jaws very powerful. Contrary to what some people think, the jaws do not lock into place and have extraordinary biting pressure. Yes, the breed has strong jaws, but there is no scientific way to measure jaw strength. The width of the head defines the jaws with a wide, square shape, and when coupled with the dog's fierce determination, there is no doubt that when an APBT decides to bite someone, it's not going to be a little nibble. Ears are either natural or cropped without wrinkles.

APBTs are heavy boned, and the dog's height and weight should look balanced. The body is a square outline and must be incredibly strong and muscular. The tail is left natural and isn't bobbed or docked. Any

The APBT features a block-like head that is wide between the ears and eyes.

coat color is allowed, including the newer merle patterns, which are dark blotches against a lighter background. Regardless of color, the coat must be short and stiff yet glossy and shiny.

Temperamental and Behavioral Aspects

The ideal APBT is a gentle giant—a loyal, intelligent, and at times very funny fellow. Come home from a long day of work, and your dog will greet you as a long-lost companion. His whole body will shake back and forth until you pet him. Devoted to many members of the family instead of just one, an APBT will never run out of love and kisses to dispense.

Aggression

Sometime around their first birthdays, APBTs begin to show aggressive tendencies toward other animals. They may fight with other dogs and chase and even kill cats and other small animals, but this aggression does not turn into people aggression. This is because when APBTs were used as fighting animals, any dog who turned

on his handler was removed from the gene pool.

To be on the safe side, try not to bring an APBT into a home that already has other pets or add other pets once you have an APBT. If you do, carefully supervise all of your pets, and if you're unable to watch them, keep the APBT separated from the other animals.

Early training and socialization is a must to curb the APBT's normal aggressiveness toward other dogs and small animals.

FAMILY-FRIENDLY TIP

APBTs and Children—Yes or No?

Are APBTs good dogs to have around children? Yes, if the children are good around the APBTs and if there is adult supervision at all times to make sure children are safe. Kids of all ages need to be taught how to behave when any dog is nearby, especially an APBT, who is born with a strong prey drive, which is a desire to chase and kill small animals. It is the parents' responsibility to teach children not to scream, run, or overexcite the dog, because he will pursue them as if they were game. An APBT is not a horse to ride, either, and wrestling or playing tug-of-war games with the dog is a big no-no.

Visiting children need to be closely supervised, too. Parents should *never* leave children alone with a dog, even for a minute. If the parents have to leave, put the dog in a safe enclosure or take him to another room.

Children shouldn't be allowed to bother the dog by jumping on him or pulling his ears and tail. APBTs have a strong pain threshold, and unlike smaller, frailer dogs, can withstand the abuse. Nevertheless, children should be taught not to treat a dog this way.

APBTs should also be taught that leaping up to grab a toy out of a child's hand and mouthing a child's hand or pant leg are unacceptable behaviors.

Companionability

Be prepared to have your APBT follow you from room to room. This breed is simply not happy being isolated from you and is rarely, if ever, aloof. APBTs are ready, willing, and able to join you in just about any game and will continually entice you into play by fetching a ball or a shoe or anything handy to get your attention.

The APBT should be well socialized to curb his natural aggressiveness toward other dogs.

Why I Adore My APBT

SENIOR DOG TIP

When Is an APBT a Senior?

Most veterinarians agree that an APBT is a senior dog between seven and eight years of age. When you look at your dog at that age, you won't think of him as an oldster, because APBTs are very spry. If you care for your dog properly throughout his life, he should move into his golden years quite gracefully.

An APBT's life expectancy is about 11 to 13 years, although many live to celebrate their 15th or even 16th birthdays.

APBTs are great television watchers, too! If you are relaxing and hanging out, they will join you. In fact, napping with their heads plopped in your lap is a popular position with APBTs.

Environment

APBTs do best when they spend most of their time with you in the house and have a safe, securely fenced yard to play in. It helps to have a dog-friendly neighborhood that tolerates a slight amount of barking if a stranger rings the doorbell. Hopefully, your community welcomes all breeds and allows you to take your APBT out for a walk on a leash.

Intelligence

In the intelligence department, few breeds are smarter than APBTs, but most important, they eagerly want to please you. They have a longer attention span than most dogs do and will work

APBTs like to spend time with their human companions.

hard to understand what it is you want them to do. Once an APBT figures out what you want, move on to teaching him something else. He is bored easily and will reinvent the wheel if not challenged. Don't be surprised if your dog opens gates, doors, and drawers! If your dog sees something he wants on the top of a counter, it will seem perfectly reasonable to him to just climb up there and get it.

Having an intelligent dog doesn't always make him so easy to live with, though. Therefore, regular training is a must, and it needs to be positive yet firm. Your dog must recognize that you are in charge. If he doesn't, he'll rule the roost and make up his own rules.

Life with an American Pit Bull Terrier is always interesting and forever filled with plenty of shenanigans.

APBTs are clever and resourceful dogs who need to be challenged to keep them from becoming bored.

Chapter 2

The Stuff of

Everyday Life

An APBT is coming! Hooray! But before your companion arrives, you'll need to go shopping for some doggy supplies. It's best to have them on hand when you bring your puppy or adult dog home. This way, you'll be able to devote all of your time and energy to getting your dog settled into your household. In fact, your APBT will adjust to his new environment more smoothly if you don't have to run out for the essentials at the last minute.

Besides the basic necessities, you'll find lots of extras for sale. Save those for your wish list. The cost of pet supplies adds up quickly, so you may want to shop around before buying even the basics. You'll find puppy and adult dog paraphernalia at pet supply stores, discount stores, websites, and mail-order pet catalogs.

Bed

The crate is your dog's bed, but if you want to give him a dog cushion for the TV room, he'll probably love it. A great feature to look for in a dog bed is a cover that you can remove easily and wash.

Collar

A collar should fit your dog securely, so if you are getting a puppy, wait until you have your

Doggy Shopping List

- bed
- collar
- crate
- exercise pen
- food, water, and bowls
- grooming supplies
- identification
- leash
- toys

When fitted properly, you should be able to fit two fingers between the collar and your dog's neck.

new puppy before buying the collar. That way, you can carry him to the pet supply store and try on collars. Don't buy a size that's too big now, thinking that he will grow into it. Until he does, it can fall off his neck. Be prepared to buy a few different collars until the puppy reaches maturity.

If your new APBT is an adult dog, measure his neck and add 2 inches (5.1 cm) for the right-size collar. You should be able to fit two fingers between the collar and your dog's neck.

Choose a leather buckle or adjustable quick-release flat nylon collar. Other options are a head halter or a harness that fits around the chest. APBTs have strong necks, and it may be easier for you to control your dog with a halter or harness if he pulls at the leash. Pass up collars with spikes, because these can snag on furniture or clothing or even hurt your dog if he scratches his neck.

Crate

At first glance, a crate or pet carrier looks like a jail, but your APBT will think of it as a safe and cozy den. The crate is a great training device for housetraining or for keeping him confined and out of trouble if you can't watch him. Until he's trained to leave your possessions alone when you're

not looking, your dog needs to be in a secure area where he can't damage anything or hurt himself.

The crate will keep your puppy out of trouble if you can't watch him.

If there are other pets or children in the home, the crate is the place for him to go to get away from the crowd. It becomes your dog's sleeping quarters when you travel, and like a human seat belt, it protects him in the car in case there's an accident. Be prepared to train your dog to like the crate, but once he gets the hang of it, he'll actually prefer it.

The crate should never be used as a holding cell for punishment, nor is it a place to keep

An exercise pen gives your dog more room than a crate, but he must be supervised.

your dog if you're away from home for long hours. APBTs are intelligent and active dogs who need physical activity and mental stimulation throughout the day, and although a few hours of confinement are okay, spending all day, every day in a crate while you're away at work is unacceptable and will frustrate your dog and cause problem behaviors.

Types of Crates

You will find wire, hard-sided, and soft-sided crates, all in different shapes, sizes, and colors. Wire crates are great for hot weather because they provide good ventilation and are collapsible for easy transport. Hard-sided crates are cozy and warm when it's cold and are the only type that can be approved for airline shipping. They can be taken

18

American Pit Bull Terriers

apart for storage, but they are bulky to move. Soft-sided crates are the lightest to carry and will fold up like a suitcase. They're ideal to take on vacation, but don't leave your dog unattended in this crate. APBTs are strong and can easily scratch or chew their way out.

Choose a crate that's easy to clean and has doors and sides that fit together securely. You can use a dog cushion or a blanket to make it comfy, but if your puppy or adult dog likes to chew or tear things apart, skip the expensive bedding until he loses interest in destroying it. To give your dog something to do inside his crate, add some toys. For convenience, consider purchasing an extra crate for use in your car.

Crate Size

What size crate should you buy for an APBT? If you have a puppy and want to buy only one crate, choose a model that is high enough for an adult APBT to stand in comfortably without having to stoop over and long enough for him to easily turn around in. This may look big for a puppy, who may be tempted to eliminate in the back area of the crate, so use the panel that comes with the crate to temporarily block off the back portion.

Exercise Pen

Besides the crate, you can leave your APBT in an exercise pen for short

FAMILY-FRIENDLY TIP

Caring for the Dog Is Not Child's Play

If you think that your child should be the only one to take charge of all your dog's needs, guess again. Your son or daughter may be very responsible, and your dog may love everyone in the household, but ultimately it is the parents' responsibility to care for the family pet. This is an important job, and children are easily distracted or may even forget about feeding the dog or taking him outside to relieve himself. They're also not big enough to control a strong APBT if they're out for a walk. In fact, children can easily get hurt when the dog pulls ahead on the leash.

Younger children can begin to help you feed the dog, keep the water dish full, or do yard cleanup, but they should never be expected to perform these tasks alone. When your child is about ten years old, you can begin to give her a few dog jobs to do, such as picking up your APBT's toys or taking charge of the water dish, but be prepared to check up on her to make sure the job is done.

Licensing Your APBT

By the time your APBT is three or four months of age, many cities require dogs to be licensed with the state in which you live. The license program helps your local government monitor public health problems such as rabies and other contagious diseases, and it helps identify your dog in case he gets lost. Be sure to check with your local animal shelter about the requirements for licensing your dog. Proof that he has been vaccinated for rabies is usually required.

Unfortunately, there are some laws, known as breed-specific legislation, that affect APBTs in certain cities throughout the United States and in some countries in the rest of the world. This legislation prohibits anyone from owning, possessing, keeping, exercising, or selling an APBT. Owners are given 30 days to remove their dogs. Why did this happen? The breed has received a lot of bad publicity from illegal APBT fighting and dog-bite incidents in the home. Oftentimes, this legislation unfairly blames the breed, when it's really the owners who are responsible for their dogs' very bad behavior. To be on the safe side, research your city's ordinances before you purchase an APBT.

periods of time.

The exercise pen is ideal for a puppy. He'll have more room to move around in than in a crate, but he must be supervised. With his enormous strength, it doesn't take much for your dog to knock over the structure. Choose a strong pen that's at least 5 feet (1.5 m) tall and has a secure latch. A top cover is optional.

Food, Water, and Bowls

Before you bring your dog home, ask the breeder, rescue organization, or your veterinarian what kind of food and dog treats you should buy. (See Chapter 3 for information about dog food.)

When your dog comes home, give him bottled water instead of your tap or well water for the first few days. The minerals in water vary in different locations, and some dogs will have an upset stomach from a water source they're not accustomed to. Mix the bottled water with your tap water for a few days, and your dog's tummy will adapt to it.

Buy two bowls—one for water and one for food. You'll find inexpensive plastic, designer ceramic, and stainless steel. Although stainless steel is more expensive than the others, it will last a lifetime and is the easiest to clean. Plastic and ceramic develop hairline cracks that trap food and bacteria.

Gate

Until you are sure that your APBT will not destroy your possessions, you can

An Older Dog Comes Home

If possible, organize your schedule so that you can stay home with your new adult APBT the day you bring him home. If you can juggle another day or two off from work to spend with your dog, that's even better. He needs to bond with you and feel secure about his role in his new home. Bringing home a dog who has been shuffled around to a few different households before yours can be a challenge for him. Your APBT may be confused when he walks through your door and may think that you are just another temporary stopover.

To make him feel at ease, don't rush him! Let him take his time to feel comfortable in his new environment. Be prepared for your APBT to do a lot of sniffing around the house. He's curious about and interested in all the new sights and smells.

Slowly walk him through every room of the house, and show him the outdoor elimination area, but don't expect him to use it right away. Be patient, too, if he has a few accidents indoors during the first few days. He is learning about his environment, and it will take several days or even weeks to figure out where everything is and what is expected of him.

Introduce other family members and pets slowly the first day. Of course, everyone wants to see the new dog right away, but the attention of too many people can overwhelm him. Ask neighbors and friends to put off their visits for a few days or even weeks until you think your dog has settled in.

Unsure if your new dog has been around other dogs before? Introduce another dog on neutral territory, and make sure they are both on short leashes. Walk them alongside each other for a few blocks so that they can focus on other distractions instead of one another.

use baby or child-safety gates to block off certain rooms of your home. You'll find gates made of wood, metal, plastic, and mesh, and all of them easily attach to door frames or walls.

Grooming Supplies

APBTs may look like they don't need much grooming, but with their short, slick coat, they still need to be brushed, bathed, and have their teeth

database, the series numbers match up with the owner's name and address.

brushed and nails clipped. Shop for a rubber dog brush and a grooming glove, shampoo formulated for dogs, nail clippers or a nail grinder, and a canine toothbrush and toothpaste.

ID Tags/Microchips

In case your dog becomes lost or separated from you, an identification tag with your name and phone number will help reunite you. For a second form of identification, have your dog microchipped. Your veterinarian can insert a tiny microchip about the size of a grain of rice beneath your dog's skin between the shoulder blades. This is a painless, permanent identification. The microchip contains a series of numbers, which are read with a handheld scanner. Most veterinarians and shelters have these scanners. Stored in a

Leash

Look for a strong 4-foot (1.2 m) to 6-foot (1.8 m) leather leash ¾ inch (1.9 cm) to 1 inch (2.54 cm) wide. Avoid nylon or chain, because they aren't as strong and will hurt your hands. Don't even consider buying a retractable leash. They tangle easily and are too long and difficult to control, especially if your APBT suddenly encounters another dog. Your dog is so strong that if he takes off running, he can yank it out of your hand or even snap it.

Toys
Of all the things you need to buy, toys are the most fun. You'll find lots of stuffed toys with squeakers, but APBTs are voracious chewers and can tear these apart in no time. Be on the lookout for any pieces that your dog chews and swallows, because they can become lodged in his throat.

Setting a Schedule
Your dog needs to have a set schedule every day. Dogs like a routine because it gives them a sense of security and helps to build their confidence. By establishing regular times for meals, bathroom breaks, playtime, and naps, your dog will know what to expect. Don't worry about doing everything exactly to the minute, but the timetable shouldn't vary more than about an hour.

Indestructible hard rubber toys may be more expensive, but they last the longest and aren't likely to cause any damage.

Once you have assembled everything, it's amazing how many things one dog needs. Luckily, many of these items are one-time purchases, and they are worth the money in the long run.

Buy safe, age-appropriate toys for your APBT puppy.

The Stuff of Everyday Life

Chapter 3

Good Eating

Your APBT's overall well-being has everything to do with what he eats. Dogs have basic nutritional requirements that need to be met to sustain good health, a long life, happiness, and stable behavior. Besides the basics, every dog has his own special mealtime requests. Choosing the best dog food for your APBT can be a challenge. With so many foods available for sale, how do you know what's best for your dog?

Zero in on feeding your dog the food that best fits his needs. The surest ways to do this are to ignore the advertising you see in newspapers and magazines or hear about on television, and forget about the cost. Choose a food based on the ingredients it contains and what your dog needs for optimal performance and health.

A Balanced Diet: Nutrients

The right food for an APBT is the foundation for good health and the most important aspect of health care. Whether you select canned or dry food, choose a food that says "complete and balanced" or "nutritionally complete" on the label. This means that the ingredients have all the nutrients in the right amounts as required for each growth stage by the American Association of Feed Control Officials (AAFCO).

Balance is so important in a dog's diet that if he doesn't get enough animal protein or if the amount of nutrients is off-kilter, his health and behavior can be affected. He may become aggressive, timid, or obsessive, and he may have chronic skin or ear infections, constant shedding, a weak immune system, or gastrointestinal upsets, vomiting, or diarrhea.

Every nutrient has a specific function, and how the body uses that nutrient depends on many factors, including the dog's genetics, his age, whether or not he is under any stress, the environment, and the amount of exercise he receives.

Nutrients consist of proteins (containing 9 to 12 essential amino acids), fats, carbohydrates (including fiber), minerals (including calcium, phosphorus, magnesium, potassium, copper, sodium, chloride or chlorine, zinc, chromium, sulfur, iron, selenium, cobalt, and iodine), vitamins, and water.

Balance is very important in your dog's diet.

Sample Feeding Schedule for Each Phase of Your Dog's Life

	Puppies 8 weeks to 12 weeks	**Older Puppies** 12 weeks to 5 months	**Adolescents** 5 months to 1 year	**Adults** 1 year to 7 or 8 years	**Seniors** 7 or 8 years and older
Meals per Day	3–4	3	2–3	2	2
Recipe Formula	Puppy	Puppy	Adult	Adult	Senior

APBT puppies, like many other breeds, grow quickly. Most likely by the time your puppy is nine months old, he'll reach his total height, but he'll continue to add muscle and attain his average weight by his first birthday. While he's a growing puppy, and especially during growth spurts, he'll need twice the amount of food that he'll need later on as an adult. Your puppy will grow the most between four and seven months of age.

A quality puppy-food recipe will supply more protein, which puppies need for growth, than an adult recipe will. The protein should consist of two different animal proteins, such as chicken, turkey, duck, beef, or lamb, which are listed as the first three ingredients.

How much food should you feed your APBT at each life stage? This depends on the food you select, but dog food labels usually list a range of suggested feeding amounts.

Proteins

To find out how much protein is contained in the dog food you feed your American Pit Bull Terrier, look on the package label, but also look at what kind of protein there is. It's even more important than the amount and corresponds to your dog's activity level. Dogs are meat eaters, not vegetarians, and they need meat (or poultry) as their protein source. Because APBTs are active, busy dogs they generally need more protein than breeds do that are sedentary. Healthy sources of protein are beef, chicken, duck, turkey, venison, eggs, and lamb.

Fats

Your dog needs *polyunsaturated* fat to supply essential fatty acids, which are a cornerstone of good health. Fat has many benefits, including livening up the taste of ingredients and supplying

Carbohydrates provide your dog with energy.

energy. It's also responsible for giving your dog a shiny coat and contributes to a healthy heart. Too little polyunsaturated fat may be responsible for itching and scratching, skin lesions and growths, improper development, and a coarse, dry coat.

Carbohydrates

Carbohydrate sources in dog food are corn, barley, wheat, oats, and rice. You will also see soy listed, but though soy is high in protein, it blocks other nutrients from being absorbed. Stay away from foods that contain soy.

Dogs don't need a lot of carbohydrates, but they do need some. The digestive process breaks them down and converts them into starch and then into simple sugars and glucose, which provide energy and brain functioning.

Minerals

Minerals include calcium, phosphorus, iron, and zinc. They are coenzymes that help control biochemical reactions in the body and that are involved in the growth and regeneration of tissues. Quality dog foods generally contain more than enough minerals for your dog. Talk to your veterinarian if you are considering supplementing your dog's diet with minerals.

Vitamins

Like minerals, vitamins also function as coenzymes and play a vital role in many body processes. Vitamin A contributes to healthy eyes, skin, and coat. Vitamin B affects skin, eyes, and coat as well as the nervous system. Vitamin C helps heal tissues.

Water

Water is the most important nutrient. It regulates body temperature by releasing heat through sweating, which dogs do through their paws. Water transports waste material from the cells to the outside of the body in the form of urine and fecal matter. It also lubricates joints, intestines, and the organs of the abdomen and chest. Although food supplies a lot of your dog's water, he needs to have a clean, fresh bowl of water available at all times.

Food Labels

When you are choosing a dog food for your APBT, don't buy the brand that has the cutest television commercials or even the lowest price. Your first consideration should be what's written on the labels. There are two labels on dog food, and one should include a statement that the food meets or exceeds the nutritional guidelines that are established by the Association of American Feed Control Officials (AAFCO). The other label is a list of ingredients that contains a "guaranteed analysis." The guaranteed analysis lists the percentages of protein, fat, fiber, and water present in the food. The AAFCO requirements include 18 percent protein for adult dogs, 22 percent protein for puppies, 5 percent fat for adults, and 8 percent fat for puppies.

Somewhere on the bag, it should say that the food is complete and balanced. Choose a food that lists an animal protein source first, such as beef, chicken, turkey, or duck. Ingredients are listed from highest to lowest percentages. The second ingredient should be a grain source, such as barley, rice, oats, wheat, or corn. A different protein from the first listed should be the third one listed. Other ingredients should include carbohydrates, fats, vitamins, and minerals.

Commercial Food

Dog food manufacturers don't have to worry about designing dog food to look appetizing to dogs, but they do pay attention to the way it tastes. If dogs don't eat it, you don't buy it, so dog

A nutritionally balanced diet will keep your dog's coat looking its best

food companies are always trying to create more palatable recipes with optimal nutrition for your dog. Different recipes are available for puppies, adults, seniors, active dogs, and dogs on special diets. There are a variety of shapes and sizes, and with so many choices, it's no wonder that food shopping can be overwhelming. No doubt you have your dog's best interest at heart and want to feed him the healthiest and tastiest food you can find.

Be on the lookout for and avoid these ingredients listed on commercial food: artificial preservatives (BHA, BHT, and ethoxyquin), moisteners, artificial flavors or colors, artificial sweeteners, animal by-products, and meat if it doesn't say exactly what kind of meat it is.

Dry Food (Kibble)

How do you know what kind of dry food to buy? It may look boring to you, but dry food, otherwise known as *kibble,* is the preferred meal for APBTs. Kibble contains all the nutrition your dog needs and has many advantages. It doesn't need to be refrigerated, so you can easily take it with you if you travel with your dog. Kibble is easy to store, stays fresh for three to six months, and is less expensive in the long run, because you feed less of it than you would with canned or semi-moist foods. Another asset is that it gives your dog's mouth a workout by helping to scrape tartar off his teeth.

The disadvantage to kibble is that it is most economical when you purchase it in the largest size bag. If you have

Kibble contains all the nutrition your dog needs.

only one APBT, finding a place to store a 40-pound (20.4 kg) bag may be tricky, and it will take a while to use it up.

Don't even think of looking for bargain kibble. It's cheaper for a reason, and usually it's cheaper because the type of ingredients used is inferior to what is contained in slightly more expensive brands.

Semi-Moist Food

Semi-moist food may seem tastier to you, but you're not the one who's going to be eating it. This type of food usually contains more salt, sugar, artificial coloring agents, preservatives, and by-products than kibble does, which makes it less healthy for your dog. It is chewier than canned food and comes packaged in individual servings. Storage space is less of a problem than for dry food, although it needs to stay fresh and must be kept in the freezer or the refrigerator. Found in the freezer section of the pet-food supply store, semi-moist food is more expensive than dry food but less expensive than canned food.

Canned Food

Canned food contains some meat and vegetable ingredients, but it mostly contains water. Therefore, it takes more

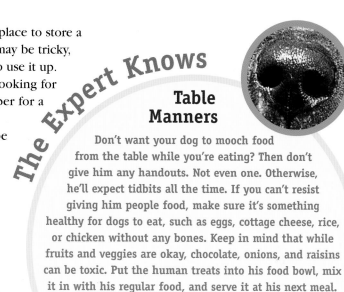

The Expert Knows

Table Manners

Don't want your dog to mooch food from the table while you're eating? Then don't give him any handouts. Not even one. Otherwise, he'll expect tidbits all the time. If you can't resist giving him people food, make sure it's something healthy for dogs to eat, such as eggs, cottage cheese, rice, or chicken without any bones. Keep in mind that while fruits and veggies are okay, chocolate, onions, and raisins can be toxic. Put the human treats into his food bowl, mix it in with his regular food, and serve it at his next meal. If you've already fed your APBT from the table, refrain from doing it again. Eventually, your dog will get the message that nothing is coming his way, and he'll give up hanging around the table while you're eating.

canned food to obtain the same amount of nutrition available in kibble. Canned food is also more expensive than kibble. There is no crunch factor in canned food, either, and APBTs like to chew their food.

If you insist on giving your APBT some canned food, the best way to use it is to mix a few tablespoons (ml) of it in with dry food.

Noncommercial Food

Many dog owners prefer to prepare their own dog food so that they can

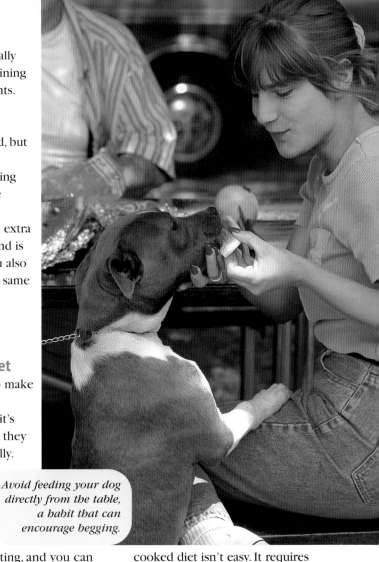

give their dog specially catered meals containing top-quality ingredients. This is the main advantage of noncommercial food, but there are a few disadvantages. Cooking up your own canine cuisine is time consuming, requires extra refrigerator space, and is more expensive. You also need to provide the same nutrients that are contained in a commercial recipe.

Homecooked Diet

Many people like to make their own dog food because they think it's healthier than what they can buy commercially. One advantage to cooking your own canine cuisine is that you know exactly

Avoid feeding your dog directly from the table, a habit that can encourage begging.

what your dog is eating, and you can provide the highest quality protein, fruit, fresh-cooked vegetables, and grains. If you like to plan meals, shop, and cook, and if you take pride in feeding your dog, making your own food can be mutually beneficial to you and your APBT.

Know in advance that a home-cooked diet isn't easy. It requires advance planning. You can't just give your dog the leftovers in your refrigerator, whatever food you can buy on sale, or the ingredients you like to eat yourself and call it healthy home-cooked dog food. The recipe you prepare should be well balanced and complete, just like a good commercial dog food. You should have two animal proteins, a fat source, carbohydrates, and the right amount of minerals, water, and vitamins.

There are a few disadvantages to making your own food. It can be difficult to take with you if you're traveling, because it needs to be refrigerated at all times. Also, the food requires storage space. It's more expensive than kibble, and obtaining fresh raw meat, including the bones, can be a challenge in some cities. You should also wear plastic gloves while you're preparing the food and be extremely diligent about keeping your kitchen counters, cutting boards, knives, food processor, plates, and storage containers bacteria-free.

To make preparation easier and to save a little money, some dog owners have formed cooperative homemade-food groups. They buy raw meat in bulk, and each person takes a turn making all the food for all the dogs in the group.

All that work can be worth it, though. After feeding their dogs a well-balanced homemade diet for some time, owners report that their dogs have more energy and that their dogs' skin and coats look better.

Raw Diet

The Bones and Raw Food or Biologically Appropriate Raw Food (BARF) diet has become very popular over the last few years. The diet consists of 60 percent raw meaty bones and 40 percent raw fruits and

FAMILY-FRIENDLY TIP

Children and Feeding

It is unfair to both your child and your dog to expect your son or daughter to be in total control of when your dog has a meal. Children are wonderful playmates, but they do not always understand the commitment it takes to feed a dog at the same time every day and in the right amounts. Instead, encourage your child to help you feed your APBT come feeding time. Ask your little one to empty the water dish and refill it with a fresh supply, pick up the dog food bowl, measure out the right amount of food, and add some water to it.

Always supervise your child when it's time to feed your APBT. Meals are often the highlight of your dog's day, and in his rush to reach the food bowl, it doesn't take much for him to accidentally knock over your child.

vegetables. A raw diet for dogs includes raw chicken and turkey (and the bones), liver, kidney, heart, brain, tongue, and tripe. Raw pureed vegetables, fresh and dried fruits, vegetable oil, brewer's yeast, kelp, apple cider vinegar, and raw honey are also included in a raw diet.

Although the BARF diet is popular with dog owners, many veterinarians aren't so enthusiastic about it. Raw meat and poultry carries the risk of E. coli and salmonella poisoning. Before you decide to feed your dog a raw diet, do some research, and talk to other dog owners who feed their dogs a raw diet to learn more about it, including safe handling techniques. Also, talk to your veterinarian. Certainly she has an opinion about whether or not you should feed your dog a raw diet and perhaps can relate the experiences of other clients who have gone this route. She'll be able to advise what's best for you and your dog.

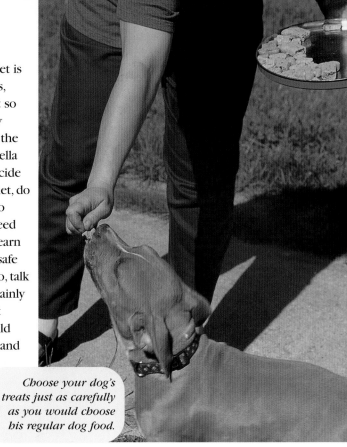

Choose your dog's treats just as carefully as you would choose his regular dog food.

Treats

Dog treats have come a long way. Where there was once just one brand of dog biscuits to buy, today there are dozens of yummy varieties everywhere you look. There's an entire aisle devoted to morsels in your local pet-food supply store, and independent bakeries specialize in making treats just for dogs. You'll find little nibbles in all different sizes, shapes, and flavors. If you still can't find an edible treasure for your dog, try making your own. Pet food cookbooks can be found in bookstores and online.

Part of the fun of having a dog is being able to give him treats to reward him during training. When your dog knows he is about to receive a special tidbit, his ears perk up, his eyes sparkle, and his tail wags happily in anticipation. What owner doesn't love seeing this reaction from her dog?

Although treats are okay to give in moderation, too many add unnecessary calories, and the wrong kinds are unhealthy. To keep them special, limit the number you hand out every day, and cut back on your dog's regular food portion to account for them. Giving out more than five to ten percent of your dog's daily food portion in extra edibles may convince your dog to pick at his kibble and hold out for the good stuff.

Don't know which treat to buy for your APBT? Choose tidbits just as carefully as you would your dog's regular dog food. Stay away from those containing chemical preservatives, artificial ingredients, food dyes, and by-products.

Supplements

When you're shopping for dog food, you'll encounter many different canine nutritional supplements. They all claim to improve the quality of your dog's life by strengthening his bones, helping him to digest his food, or giving him a shiny, thick coat.

A few of these may accomplish this, but some supplements can actually do more harm than good to your dog. Calcium supplements, for example, promote bone growth, but good-quality dog foods already contain calcium. Giving too much calcium can be dangerous. The last

thing you want to have happen to your APBT puppy is for him to grow too much too fast, because this may lead to hip dislocation.

Commercial dog foods today are far better than they once were, and they contain everything your dog needs. If you stick to feeding your dog a well-balanced, quality dog food, no supplements are necessary. However, you should consult your veterinarian if you think your dog might need supplementation in his diet.

Free Feeding Versus Scheduled Feeding

Free feeding your APBT means filling your dog's food bowl with the day's allotment of food, putting the bowl down, and leaving it all day. This may not be the best choice for your dog for a few reasons. After food sits for more than a half-hour, it begins to look unappetizing. Besides, if you have only

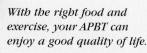

With the right food and exercise, your APBT can enjoy a good quality of life.

SENIOR DOG TIP

Feeding the Older Dog

Your veterinarian may recommend switching your APBT to a special senior recipe dog food when he's seven to eight years old. Senior dog food has fewer calories and less protein and is specially formulated for the nutritional needs of older dogs.

Some senior APBTs lose enthusiasm for meals and become a little too thin. To encourage your dog to eat more to put on some weight, enhance the flavor of his food by adding some beef or chicken broth, macaroni and cheese, or a little meat.

he feels like it. Eating all day long makes him lethargic and less interested in running around, and before you know it, your dog may become obese. If you have a multiple-dog household and you leave the food down, one dog may get all of it and another might lose out completely. There is no way to control the amounts each dog gets.

There may come a time when you will take your dog on vacation with you or when you will need to board him. Free feeding him in these situations won't be a consideration, and your dog will suddenly have to adapt to a new food regimen, which may be confusing to him.

Feeding your dog at scheduled mealtimes is the way to go for an APBT. With this method, you are able to control how much your dog eats at each meal, and you can vary the amount you give him depending upon his weight. For the easiest digestion, veterinarians recommend feeding adult dogs twice a day.

When you feed your dog, leave the food down for 15 minutes. If he doesn't finish it in that length of time and walks away from it, pick up the bowl and dump the food out. Don't give him anything until his next regularly scheduled mealtime. Then, feed him the regular amount. Eventually, he'll get the message that if he doesn't eat at mealtime, he won't get food until mealtime rolls around again.

one dog and he doesn't eat it all, it can attract bugs and spoil, especially if it's a warm day.

Another reason that free feeding is a bad idea is that you have no way of knowing if your dog is sick or not. Refusing to eat is a sign that your dog is ill, and if there is food in the bowl all the time, you may not know until it's too late that your dog isn't eating.

Leaving the food down all the time encourages your dog to eat whenever

Obesity

Having an overweight APBT is a serious problem. Overweight dogs are prone to cardiovascular disease, kidney disease, and joint problems, and the extra pounds (kg) can shorten his life.

To check if your dog is obese, stand next to him and look down at his overall outline. You should see a slightly hourglass-shaped figure. Run your hands over his sides, and you should be able to feel his ribs without pressing too hard. The ribs shouldn't stick out, and his stomach should be slightly tucked up without any rolls of fat.

To put your APBT on a diet, consult your veterinarian. She may recommend that you gradually cut back on the amount of food you give him while increasing his exercise. Take him walking, or toss the ball around several times during the day. APBTs enjoy being active every day, especially if the activity is fun. Whether it's romping through the park, chasing a flying disk, or jogging around the block, be prepared to spend an hour a day exercising your dog.

As APBTs age, their metabolism slows down and their dietary needs change. Senior dogs aren't as active as they once were, but if they continue to eat the same amount as they did when they were younger, they will be chubby in no time. Being overweight isn't healthy, because it can cause heart problems and joint and feet injuries.

To keep your older dog from getting too fat in his golden years, try cutting back a little on how much you regularly feed him. If your dog seems really hungry after eating less, try feeding him some low-calorie, high-fiber dog food, which will help fill him. There are many commercial low-calorie dog food recipes offering 15 percent fewer calories per pound (kg). You can also give your dog some vegetables to eat, which won't add any extra calories. Lightly steam some fresh green beans, broccoli, and sliced carrots, or give your APBT a few tablespoonfuls (ml) of canned pumpkin to lower his caloric intake and help balance out his meals.

With the right food and exercise, it's not hard to keep your APBT healthy, especially if you enjoy taking him out for a daily walk or jog. Keep an eye on his overall weight, because this is a breed that likes to eat. Sure, it's hard to look at the pleading eyes of your APBT and pass up giving him a treat or two, but if you want to have him for as long as possible, saying no is the best thing you can do for him.

Chapter 4

Looking Good

With his smooth, muscular, clean-cut look, the APBT doesn't need a lot of fussy grooming or expensive trips to a groomer, but there are a few things you will need to do to keep him spruced up. Begin when your dog is a puppy and he will look forward to having a bath, being brushed, and getting his nails trimmed. If you have an adult dog, give him a few days to settle into your household before his first grooming session.

Even the shorthaired APBT needs regular care to keep him healthy. Keeping his ears and teeth clean is good preventive maintenance. With regular upkeep, you can catch any problems before they become bigger health issues.

It helps to have the right tools, and to make the job even easier, gather all your grooming supplies ahead of time and keep them in one place. That way, you'll have them handy when you are ready to groom.

Coat and Skin Care

At first glance, the APBT's coat looks like there's no maintenance involved. However, this is an incorrect assumption. Even if he spends most of his time indoors, his short and bristled hair will have a slightly doggy odor to it. Add in digging outdoors or rolling in the dirt, which he loves to do, and your dog will definitely smell like the great outdoors. Being a wash-and-wear breed, it takes less than an hour or two to brush your dog, check him for any health problems, give him a bath, towel-dry him or use a dryer, and clean his ears and eyes. In no time at all, you can return your dog's coat to its former glossy condition.

Brushing

Should you bathe your dog and then brush him? Or should you brush first and bathe later? Unless you want a lot of wet dog hair all over your house,

American Pit Bull Terriers

Grooming Supplies

- medium- to soft-bristle dog brush for brushing and removing dander and dirt
- rubber curry brush to remove loose hair
- flea comb
- nonslip bath mat
- quality shampoo and conditioner made especially for dogs
- large cotton towels and washcloths (one or two) or high-speed dog dryer
- handheld shower spray attachment
- canine toothbrush and toothpaste
- nail clippers or nail grinder
- styptic powder
- rolled cotton or cotton balls
- ear cleaner available from your veterinarian
- ophthalmic ointment

brush first and then bathe. You can even brush your dog with a medium-bristle brush without bathing him. Daily brushing will cut down on how much your dog sheds (even short, bristle-haired dogs shed a little), because it helps stimulate the natural oils in the coat, which give it a sleek and glossy appearance. It also removes dirt, dander, and loose hairs.

How to Brush Your APBT

To brush your dog, apply light pressure and use the bristle brush. Begin brushing at the top of your dog's neck and continue down his back. Don't forget his chest, shoulders, legs, and tail. You need to brush for only a few minutes. Lightly go over his cheeks and the top of his head. Next, use the rubber curry brush to add some polish and to catch any other dead hair. When you're not using the rubber brush, be sure to keep it away from your dog's reach. APBTs love to chew the rubber!

To check for the presence of any fleas, use a flea comb. Comb through the hair under your dog's tail, on his rump, along his back and chest, and on top of his head. If you don't see any fleas, check to see if there are any tiny dark

Regular grooming will keep your APBT's coat clean and shiny.

specks that look like pepper. These are flea droppings and they mean that your dog has fleas.

When you're through brushing and combing, use a damp cloth to wipe all the loose hair off your dog. For an extra shine, use a spritz of mink oil spray to smooth down the coat and to give your dog a fresh, clean smell. You can find mink oil spray at pet-food supply stores, usually in the shampoo department.

Bathing

After a good brushing, your APBT is ready for a good scrubbing. Whether you have a puppy or an older dog, take your time when you introduce the bath experience, and resist rushing him into the water.

Before you begin the spa treatment, first take your dog outdoors to relieve himself. You don't want him to get his feet dirty first thing once he's clean.

Since there's no telling ahead of time if your pup will love taking a bath or think it's the worst idea in the world, plan on making this a positive

Grooming as a Health Check

A spruce-up session with your dog is a great time to thoroughly check him over for signs of any health problems. When he's up on a table, carefully inspect his body for any scratches or unusual lumps that could be cancerous or any open wounds that have either suddenly cropped up or that haven't healed. If you find anything you're concerned about, take your APBT to the veterinarian for a checkup. You may discover a condition that needs treatment before it becomes worse.

Check for fleas, and if you find only a few, ask your veterinarian for a flea preventive immediately, before fleas have a chance to multiply and overrun your dog's coat. Inspect your dog for ticks that may be hiding in the ears, neck, or rear, or foxtails, which are sharp bristles and pieces of dried grass embedded in your dog's chest, feet, or ears. Remove any ticks (see Chapter 5), and pluck off any foxtails yourself before they work their way deeper into your dog's skin and cause problems. Inspect your dog's feet for splinters, torn toenails, or ragged footpads that may signal a trip to the veterinarian. In addition, the eyes and ears should be clear. Any redness or strange discharges may signal an infection.

experience. To increase the chance that he will take to the water, choose a day and time when it isn't too cold, because puppies and even adult APBTs can chill easily. If you're bathing your dog outdoors, use warm water. No one likes getting wet when they're cold, even your dog. Make sure, too, that you're not rushed at bath time. Your puppy may need some extra tender loving care in order to feel comfortable in the tub.

Pre-Bath Prep

To get ready to give your dog a bath, gather all your bathing supplies before you put him into the tub. Nothing is worse than getting your dog all soaped up and suddenly realizing you don't have anything to dry him off with. Sure enough, the minute you step out of the bathroom to get a towel, your wet dog will jump out of the tub and shake himself until the walls and floor are covered with soapy water. Last, lay a towel on the bathroom floor next to the tub so that your dog can stand securely without slipping.

How to Bathe Your APBT

With a puppy or a new adult dog, begin with mini sponge baths. Just fill the tub with enough warm—never hot or cold—water to wash your dog's legs. Put your dog inside the tub on a bath mat, and keep one hand under his chin. Use your other hand to wet his feet, put a little shampoo on his legs, and rinse him with the handheld shower sprayer. Your dog may wiggle around a lot, so hold him gently in place until you're done bathing him. If he gives you a really hard time struggling to jump out of the tub, there are rubber leashes you can buy that attach to the tub wall and hold your dog in place.

This is a wash-and-go bath experience, so lift your dog out and dry his feet off with a towel after just a few minutes. When he's dry, give him a little food treat and tell him, "Good boy!" In subsequent baths, wash him a little more each time.

When your APBT is ready for a complete bath, start by spraying one side of his body and his back with water, and then add a little shampoo. Don't forget his chest, tummy, and tail! With most dog shampoos, a little goes a long way. Using the rubber brush, work up a lather and then rinse it off. Be sure to get all the soap out, because any residue will cause itchiness and flaky, dry skin. When you're through with one

side, turn him around and repeat the process. If your dog's coat seems dry, use a little conditioner, but you probably won't need to add it every time.

Save washing your APBT's head for the end. Use a wet washcloth to wipe his face and the top of his head. Try not to get water or soap in your dog's eyes or ears! If you do, rinse it out completely so that it doesn't burn.

In no time at all, the bath will be over. Now comes the fun part. Take a towel and put it on top of your dog before taking him out of the tub. That way, if he starts shaking himself, the water won't become airborne. If he's light enough to lift, place his feet onto the towel on the floor. Dry him completely so that he doesn't become chilled.

How often should you give your APBT a bath? It all depends on how dirty he gets and how much of a doggy odor you can tolerate. If your APBT smells really bad, he may have an infection or a skin problem. Chances are it went undetected because a layer of dirt covered it up! Here's where a bath

comes in handy. When your dog's skin is clean, you'll be able to spot any deep scratches, wounds, or lumps and take him to the veterinarian for treatment. Like human hair, a clean APBT coat is a healthy coat.

A bath about once every two to four weeks usually does the job. Don't worry about his skin getting too dry from regular bathing. Today's canine shampoos are specially formulated to retain moisture and add extra oils that are beneficial for the skin.

If your dog has just a spot or two of dirt you'd like to remove, but he doesn't need a full-scale bath, you can always use waterless shampoo. It's great for touch-up jobs!

Nail Care

It's a fact. Dogs' nails grow. And grow. Even if your dog runs a lot on pavement, there's no guarantee that his nails will stay short. Some dogs naturally have shorter nails than others. Your job is to make sure that your dog's nails don't grow so long that they hit the ground and make a clicking sound when he walks across the floor. When this happens, it forces the toes to spread out and can throw your APBT off balance. You might not think that long toenails could be responsible for a dog going lame, but that's exactly what can happen. To keep your dog's feet in good condition, clip his nails once a week. If

To keep your dog's feet in good condition, clip his nails once a week.

you have a puppy, start clipping his nails as soon as you bring him home. If you have an adult dog, it's never too late to begin.

How to Trim Your APBT's Nails

Although some dogs don't mind their nails being trimmed and will stand patiently while the job is being done, other APBTs don't like someone handling their toes. Be persistent, and he'll get the message that this is necessary. Training your dog to like his nails being trimmed may take some time, but the effort is worth it. Begin by simply picking up each foot every day—even a few times a day—and gently massaging the foot and toes. You can even give him a food treat while you're handling his feet. Soon he'll realize that you touching his feet is perfectly fine.

The next step is to gather the trimming tools you'll need. Pour a little styptic powder into the cap of its bottle. (Styptic powder will stop the bleeding in case you cut your dog's nail too short.) Hopefully, you won't need to use it, but if you do, having it ready is helpful.

Next, lift one foot and trim one nail. If your APBT doesn't make a fuss, give him a treat and tell him, "Good dog!" Clip a few more nails, but don't try to do all of them during the first session. If he struggles, don't take him off the table right away. Instead, wait until he settles down for a few minutes before you put him back on the ground. You don't want him to think that if he fusses enough,

The Grooming Table

Putting your APBT on a dog-grooming table that has a grooming-arm attachment makes brushing him and trimming his nails much easier. The grooming arm has a noose for your dog's head, which keeps him in place. You can also use an outdoor picnic table or any sturdy table you have around the house if it is waist high. When your dog is on the table, he will be less inclined to move around, and you don't have to get down on the ground and lean over him to get the job done. Most tables have a nonskid surface and fold up easily for storage.

Don't leave your dog alone on the table or turn your back on him—even for a minute—because he can easily slip and fall off.

you'll quit. Continue massaging his feet for a few minutes every day.

If you are new to nail clipping, you may feel nervous that you'll cut the nail too deeply into the quick, which is the nail core of blood vessels and nerve endings, and it will bleed. If this happens, quickly dip the nail into the styptic powder in the bottle cap. Don't worry. Your dog is not going to bleed to death, and he won't be ruined for life. It happens on occasion, even to the best groomers. The more often you clip nails, the better you'll get at it.

You should clip your APBT's nails once a week, before they have a chance to grow out too much. This way, you'll have less work to do each time.

Ear Care

Bath time is a good opportunity to clean your dog's ears, but don't wait until then. Get in the habit of picking up your dog's earflaps and examining them every day for any foul odor, discharge, inflammation, or black waxy debris. Be on the lookout, too, if your dog scratches his ears or shakes or tilts his head a lot. These are signs that your dog may have an ear infection. If so, you can clean out what's inside the ears and prevent the problem from getting worse.

If you suspect your dog has an ear infection, you can clean what's inside the ears and prevent the problem from getting worse.

How to Clean Your APBT's Ears

To clean the ears, assemble everything you need before you call your dog to you, including opening the ear cleaning solution and tearing the cotton into short strips. Once you and your APBT are ready, it helps to sit down and hold on to your dog's collar. Your dog can either sit or stand. Using your other hand, pick up the earflap and hold the ear back at the tip. Quickly squirt in some ear cleaner. If you take too long doing this, your dog will lose his patience, because the solution tickles. Massage the ear at the base, back and forth until you hear the liquid squishing around inside, almost like a washing machine. Take one of the cotton strips and push it down as far as you can into the car canal. Don't worry about going too far, because the ear canal is way below your reach. Twist it around so that it catches the debris along the inside, and take it out. If you see a lot of black waxy buildup, repeat the process. You may have to apply the solution and wipe out the ear a few times before the cotton comes out clean. Don't use cotton swabs, as these only push the debris down without extracting it.

Eye Care

Compared with other breeds, APBTs are not known to have hereditary eye problems. Still, it's a good idea to look closely at them during your regular grooming session.

How to Clean Your APBT's Eyes

If you notice a green or yellow discharge in the corners of your dog's eyes, wipe it away with a cotton ball dipped into warm water. If you see the discharge again, call your veterinarian, as a green or yellow coloration may signal an infection. Normal mucus is clear or black.

Dental Care

As on human teeth, plaque builds up on canine teeth. If it isn't removed, it hardens into tartar, which causes an infection in the gums and progresses to tooth decay. If your dog has bad breath, chances are his teeth need cleaning.

How to Clean Your APBT's Teeth

To keep canine choppers plaque-free, brush them at least once or twice a week, although every day is better. Use a canine toothbrush and toothpaste made especially for dogs. Human toothpaste can upset your dog's stomach if he swallows it. Dog toothpaste doesn't need to be rinsed, because it dissolves inside the canine mouth. Dogs really like the taste of it, too!

Brushing your dog's teeth isn't hard once you and your dog get the hang of it. Set aside one to two minutes every day, and begin with your dog in a sitting position. Let him sniff the toothbrush. Then, put some toothpaste on your finger. When he tastes it, gently rub your finger over a few of his teeth. Repeat this a few more times until he's comfortable with your fingers and the toothpaste in his mouth. This may take a few days.

When you feel that your APBT is

47

A daily tooth inspection and brushing promotes good oral hygiene.

SENIOR DOG TIP

Grooming the Older Dog

As APBTs age, it becomes even more important to keep their nails trimmed short and their ears, eyes, and teeth cleaned regularly. Senior dogs are not as sure-footed as they once were, and they may lose their balance. Nails that are too long hamper their walking ability even more. In later years, ears tend to have greater waxy buildup, eyes have more of a discharge, and tartar forms faster.

There is something soothing about taking care of an older dog. It's your chance to give him some special attention and to reconnect with how much joy he has brought you over the years. Your reward? Some special kisses from your special fellow.

ready for the toothbrush, put some toothpaste on it, gently lift his lip, and slowly brush one or two front teeth in a circular pattern. Don't try to brush the whole mouth all at once.

At the next session, brush a few more teeth, including the ones in back, as these are the ones that are most likely to have periodontal disease. Work up to brushing all the teeth. Stop brushing before your dog begins to wiggle around. Otherwise, he'll learn that if he fusses, you'll stop probing his mouth.

Finding a Professional Groomer

If you decide that grooming your APBT is more than you want to tackle on your own, you can always take him to a professional groomer. Besides having the appropriate equipment, a reputable groomer is experienced and knows how to handle different kinds of dogs. You may, however, encounter a groomer who is uncomfortable around APBTs and may not want to do the job. If so, it's best to find out before taking him in. When you're interviewing groomers, inquire right away whether or not they accept APBTs.

To find a conscientious groomer who will give your APBT a beauty makeover, ask your veterinarian, breeder, or friends for names of people they recommend. Important questions to pose to groomers should include what kind of training or experience they have, if they hold a valid dog-grooming business license, and what other services besides bathing they provide, such as cleaning ears, brushing teeth, clipping toenails, and expressing anal glands.

It's also helpful to find out if they are comfortable handling dogs who are large and strong, what shampoos and conditioners they use, and if they use towels, a hand-held dryer, or a standing

cage dryer. When a stand-up cage dryer is used, no one has to hold it. However, be sure to find out if someone checks on the dog while the dryer's hot air blows on him, so that your APBT doesn't overheat.

Will the groomer put a muzzle on your dog or give him sedatives if she feels it is necessary? If so, you may not want your dog to have medication without a veterinarian administering it, as it may be harmful. You also want to know how long it will take to have your dog groomed. If it's longer than four hours, find out if your APBT will be taken outside to relieve himself and if the dog walker is strong enough to handle him. Ask, too, if the area where the dogs eliminate is fenced so that

you don't have to worry what will happen to your dog if he gets loose.

Visit the establishment before making the first appointment. Look for clean and organized facilities with safe, roomy crates for the dogs who are waiting to be groomed or are finished.

Once you and your dog get the hang of the whole grooming routine, you'll both enjoy spending that quality time together. It's a chance for you to devote a regular hour each week to fuss over your APBT and an opportunity for him to bask in all the extra attention. This positive bonding experience carries over into training time. Your dog trusts you and will be eager to follow your instructions.

Chapter 5

Feeling Good

One look at the muscular APBT and it's easy to think, "Here's one hardy breed!" Then again, even if an APBT was ill, you might never even know it. APBTs have a high tolerance for pain and often don't react to feeling out of sorts until the illness is serious or it's too late to obtain medical attention.

To maintain good health, it takes an observant owner to recognize when an ABPT is feeling well or suffering in silence. In fact, knowing the symptoms of illnesses that APBTs may develop will help you spot a problem early on and seek treatment before it's too late.

Finding a Veterinarian

Having a skillful veterinarian with whom you and your dog feel comfortable can make all the difference in your APBT's health. To locate a good veterinarian, ask other dog owners, your breeder, or rescue coordinator for referrals. In addition, your local chamber of commerce will also have a list of reputable veterinarians in your community whom you can interview.

When searching for a veterinarian, inquire if the doctor is comfortable handling your breed, how many APBTs she has treated, and if she is familiar with APBT health problems and wellness. An office that is nearby is convenient. If after-hours care is provided, that's a bonus, but most veterinarians today refer patients to an emergency clinic with which they confer.

Ask how many veterinarians are on staff. More than one veterinarian means that a veterinarian is always available during office hours. You should also visit the office before your dog has a problem, so that you can meet with a veterinarian and see if the facility is clean and safe.

Inquire about what training the veterinary technicians have and how long they have worked at the office. It's

It takes an observant owner to recognize when an APBT is feeling ill.

FAMILY-FRIENDLY TIP

Preparing Your Child for a Vet Visit

If your child is old enough to walk beside you without having to be carried, and can understand that a veterinary office is no place to run around or make a lot of noise in, then your son or daughter is old enough to accompany you and your APBT on a visit to the veterinarian. If this isn't the case, find a babysitter. It's too difficult to manage a toddler and an APBT who both demand your attention. In a crowded waiting room, other dogs may want to challenge yours, and to avoid a possible altercation, you'll need to focus on your dog at all times.

If, on the other hand, your child is physically and mentally mature enough to accompany you and your APBT to the vet, talk to your son or daughter about what to expect at the office before you leave home. Explain that other dogs may not be as friendly as your APBT is, and that if he or she wants to pet a dog there, to ask the owner for permission. Since the visit may seem like a long time to a child, suggest bringing a small, quiet toy or book from home to keep busy with.

Stress how great it is to have your child's help with your dog so that he or she feels like a part of the healing process. Mention, too, that your dog may not be happy to be there and may not be the same lovable fellow he is at home who likes to be petted. Therefore, it may be best to leave the dog alone while the veterinarian is examining him. Explain that your dog may cry during an examination but that he's in good hands with the veterinarian.

Feeling Good

reassuring if they are knowledgeable and enjoy working with dogs and the veterinarians at the facility.

Regular Veterinary Visits

APBTs need regular annual checkups, just like people do. During an exam, the veterinarian can spot a potential problem that may be prevented with the right care. Once a year, your dog will need a blood test to make sure he doesn't have heartworm.

At the same time, your veterinarian can give your dog a routine examination. She will check your dog's weight and temperature, as well as his eyes, ears, mouth, skin, and coat. The veterinarian will also listen to your APBT's heart and lungs and examine his anal glands.

A routine office visit is a good opportunity for you to discuss any concerns you have about your dog's health or behavior. If your veterinarian thinks that more information is needed to make a diagnosis, she may recommend a blood test, an electrocardiogram, urine collection, or x-rays.

Don't be afraid to ask in advance what the costs will be.

Neutering (Spaying and Castrating)

One of the kindest things you can do for your APBT is to have your male castrated (removing the testicles) or your female spayed (removing the ovaries and uterus). These procedures have many health benefits, although reducing the risk of cancers of the reproductive system is the biggest one.

Surely you love your dog and wouldn't want him to have prostate cancer or her to have mammary cancer or uterine infections. If females are spayed before their first season, usually by six months of age, there is less risk that they will develop breast cancer. When males are castrated before they are a year old, there's a good chance they may not have prostate problems later on. Males will have less of a desire to sneak out of the house searching for females in season, as well as reduced aggression toward other dogs. Females won't have heat cycles, so you won't have a mess at home to clean up.

Another good reason for neutering is not having puppies and contributing to the pet overpopulation problem. There are hundreds of APBTs who are abandoned and euthanized each year because no one wants them. Adding more puppies when there are so many who already need homes is unconscionable.

Unless you are planning to breed your APBT, it is best to have him neutered.

Dogs should receive a series of vaccinations beginning when they are six to eight weeks old.

Vaccinations

Dog owners don't usually look forward to giving their dogs vaccines, but the fact is that they save lives. Although veterinarians and vaccine manufacturers don't always agree about which vaccines dogs should be given and how often, the American Animal Hospital Association (AAHA) Canine Vaccine Task Force and the American Veterinary Medical Association (AVMA) Council on Biologic and Therapeutic Agents have established vaccination guidelines. These guidelines advise that canine distemper virus, canine parvovirus, canine adenovirus-2, and rabies are serious diseases against which dogs should be

vaccinated. Puppies should have a series of these vaccinations beginning when they are 6 to 8 weeks old, continuing at 9 to 11 weeks and 12 to 14 weeks, and ending at about 16 weeks. They need a booster when they are one year old and again every three years.

Traditionally, all vaccines were given once a year, but today, many veterinarians and owners prefer to check a dog's immunity levels annually with antibody titers before giving a vaccine. Often a dog already has enough immunity against a disease and doesn't need a vaccine.

There are other vaccines recommended for diseases such as

canine parainfluenza, leptospirosis, bordetella (kennel cough), and Lyme disease if a dog's lifestyle, geographic location, or travel put him at risk. Three additional vaccines are available, although optional, against giardia, canine coronavirus, and canine adenovirus-1, because these diseases are not as threatening. Be sure to discuss with your vet any concerns you have about giving your dog vaccines.

The following are some diseases that some veterinarians recommend vaccinating against.

Bordetella (Kennel Cough)

If you hear your dog gagging or hacking, chances are he has kennel cough. An upper respiratory disease that is highly contagious, this disease is more aggravating than serious. A nasal spray vaccine prevents some of the strains, and kennels require dogs to have it prior to being boarded. Your dog should also have the nasal spray once every six months if he's going to be around other dogs, either in training classes or at dog shows. There is no cure for this disease—only supportive treatment. In some cases, antibiotics may be used.

Coronavirus

This disease is transmitted through contact with infected oral and fecal secretions. The early signs are depression, loss of appetite, vomiting, fever, and diarrhea. The stool is yellow-orange, foul smelling, watery, and sometimes bloody. Your veterinarian can treat the disease with fluid and electrolyte replacement, as well as antibiotics.

Distemper

Unvaccinated puppies may contract distemper, which is often fatal. Symptoms include upper respiratory problems, fever, vomiting, diarrhea, and neurological conditions.

Giardia

APBTs develop giardia after drinking from contaminated outdoor water sources. This is why it's so important to take your own water with you when you travel with your dog. Symptoms include bloody stools, diarrhea, weight loss, and bloating. Your veterinarian can treat the problem with an antibiotic.

Leptospirosis

Leptospirosis is spread when dogs eat something that is contaminated by an infected animal. It is found in outdoor water sources, such as lakes, ponds, and streams inhabited by livestock or rats. This disease damages the liver and kidneys. Look for signs of bloody diarrhea or urine, lethargy, vomiting, loss of appetite, excessive thirst, bloodshot eyes, and mouth eruptions. Treatment consists of antibiotics.

Lyme Disease

A tick with Lyme disease transmits the disease to a dog through its saliva. These ticks are small, so it may be more difficult to see them, but they are usually attached for two days before they infect a dog. Symptoms include lethargy, weakness, feverishness, and lameness. This disease can be treated with antibiotics.

Parainfluenza

This is a combination of several different viruses and a bacteria. If your dog is suffering from parainfluenza, he will be weak and have a dry, hacking cough. Fortunately, the disease is not fatal, and your veterinarian can give your dog an antibiotic to treat it.

Dogs can suffer from allergies, just as humans can.

Parvovirus

Extremely contagious and fatal, parvovirus affects the stomach lining, bone marrow, and lymph nodes. It is transmitted through contaminated stools. Early signs include vomiting, bloody diarrhea, and fever. Keep an eye on a young puppy. If he suddenly becomes lethargic and doesn't want to eat, he may have parvovirus. He will need to see the veterinarian immediately. Treatment includes antibiotics and fluids given intravenously to prevent dehydration.

Rabies

State laws require dogs to be vaccinated against rabies because it is fatal to dogs and dangerous to people. The vaccination should be given once every three years in some states and once a year or every other year in other states. It affects the nervous system, and dogs contract the disease from other dogs who have it. Watch for signs of sudden aggression or lethargy. If your dog has a fever and you notice his facial muscles contracting, take him to the veterinarian immediately.

Breed-Specific Health Issues in APBTs

All dogs—pure or mixed breed—inherit diseases from their ancestors and pass on defective genes from one generation to the next. Fortunately, APBTs have fewer health issues than most other breeds. Being aware of what they are will enable you to obtain medical help for your APBT right away or to take some precautions to lessen their severity.

Allergies

APBTs can suffer from allergies, which are side effects caused by the immune system. A dog can be allergic to many things, such as pollens, molds, house dust, insect bites, certain foods, drugs, and chemicals. Exposure to them triggers a reaction that can include itching, sneezing, coughing, tearing, vomiting, or diarrhea. To be allergic to something in food or in the environment, a dog must be exposed to it at least twice.

If you notice intense scratching and red, swollen skin, your dog may be allergic to fleabites. There are flea products available through your veterinarian that will rid your dog of fleas. For other problems that you suspect may be due to allergies, keep a log of your dog's symptoms, and contact your veterinarian. The information you collect will help her diagnose the problem. She may refer you to a veterinary allergy specialist who can perform further testing and determine the exact cause of the allergy.

Bloat/Gastric Torsion

In deep-chested breeds like the APBT, bloat, or gastric torsion, is a serious and often fatal health concern. With bloat, the stomach becomes distended from gas or water or both, and it swells and twists. Bloat happens suddenly and can kill a dog within a few hours. It is not known exactly how the condition is caused, but many suspect that gulping down a large meal or large bowl of water, vigorous exercise too soon after eating, and stress can contribute to the problem. Male dogs over the age of two years with deep chests seem to be more affected than females.

A dog emergency happens quickly, and you need to be prepared. Keeping a first-aid kit handy will help your dog until you can transport him to your veterinarian or after-hours clinic.

Here's what you'll need:

- number of national poison control center
- your veterinarian's phone number—even if you know it, during an emergency you may not be able to remember it
- after-hours emergency clinic phone number
- antibiotic ointment—to use in a wound after it's been cleaned
- antidiarrheal medication—if the diarrhea lasts more than a day, see your veterinarian
- antiseptic and antibacterial baby cleansing wipes

- antihistamine—in case of bee stings and spider bites; contact your veterinarian for dosage
- digital rectal thermometer—you may need to know your APBT's temperature
- ear cleaner—for routine care
- hydrogen peroxide 3% solution (USP)—for cleaning wounds and wiping away blood
- instant cold compress—to cool your dog down from overheating
- latex gloves—for your protection against contamination
- muzzle or gauze roll—to wrap around your dog's muzzle to prevent him from accidentally biting you if in pain
- nonstick adhesive tape or vet wrap—more comfortable than tape for keeping gauze bandages in place
- rubbing alcohol—to clean the thermometer before and after using it
- saline eye solution—to flush eyes
- small scissors—to cut bandages
- sterile cotton balls, rolled cotton, or cotton strips—for ear cleaning or wiping out a wound
- sterile gauze pads—to stop bleeding and cover wounds
- towels and washcloths—to wash any wounds
- tweezers—for removing ticks
- veterinary first-aid manual

Be on the lookout for these signs: abdominal swelling and lethargy, excessive salivation, rapid breathing, pale and cool skin in the mouth, and a dazed look. Call your veterinarian and transport your dog to her office or an emergency clinic immediately. Your veterinarian can perform a surgical procedure to prevent recurrence.

Canine Hip Dysplasia (CHD)

In dogs suffering from CHD, the thigh bone doesn't fit correctly into the pelvic socket, making the hip joint loose. This causes a painful, wobbly gait in most dogs, but APBTs have a high pain tolerance, and some may seem to ignore the discomfort, although the pain is intense. Using hip x-rays, the condition is evaluated and rated by the Orthopedic Foundation for Animals (OFA) and the Pennsylvania Hip Improvement Program (PennHIP).

Many breeds suffer from CHD, a crippling inherited health problem, but APBTs are particularly affected.

According to the OFA, over the past few years, 20 percent of all APBT x-rays were judged to be dysplastic.

If you are buying a puppy, ask the breeder if the parents' hips have been x-rayed and if they are free from hip dysplasia. If so, you have a better chance of acquiring a dog who will not develop the problem when he grows up. Although parent dogs with normal hips may produce offspring with hip dysplasia, the chances of that happening are low.

Cruciate Tears and Ruptures

APBTs are active, athletic dogs who are prone to rupturing their stifle joints from too much running and jumping. (Think of a football player sidelined because of a knee injury.) If you notice your dog limping on a rear leg or not moving around much at all, contact your veterinarian. It is likely that your dog will need surgery to repair it.

Hypothyroidism

Many breeds are diagnosed with hypothyroidism, which is a thyroid hormone deficiency that can affect your APBT's metabolism. A wide range of symptoms may occur, including weight gain, lethargy, hair loss, and infertility. Your veterinarian can diagnose this

APBTs are athletic dogs who are prone to rupturing their stifle joints from too much running and jumping.

condition with a blood test, and if indicated, thyroid replacement drugs can stabilize the thyroid level.

Impacted Anal Glands

If you notice your dog scooting his rear along the carpet, it usually means that his anal glands are clogged. Located on each side of the anus, they produce a liquid that lubricates the rectum, enabling your dog to propel stool through.

To ease the condition, your veterinarian can clean out your dog's anal glands. Ask your veterinarian to demonstrate the procedure so that you can do it yourself the next time. You can also try giving your dog a tablespoon (ml) of canned pumpkin (not pie spice mix) in his food, or add some fiber, such as lightly steamed broccoli or green beans, to his diet.

If you see blood or pus in the stool, contact your veterinarian, because there may be an infection.

Skin Problems

If your dog is scratching and licking himself constantly, it is possible that he may be developing an allergic skin reaction. APBTs are especially prone to suffering from this problem. Harmful food ingredients, the wrong shampoo, the environment, or stress might be the cause. Your veterinarian can evaluate your dog's condition and possibly suggest feeding your dog a different food, changing his bedding, or giving him medication to reduce the itching.

General Illnesses

It's a fact that dogs get sick. Your goal is to minimize or prevent illness as much as possible so that your APBT can live a long and healthy life. Of course, prevention is the best way to safeguard your dog's wellness. It also helps to be aware of any changes in your dog's health, because the sooner you seek help for your dog if he is ill, the better his chances are of recovery. Keep an ongoing log of any symptoms

If your APBT is constantly scratching at himself, he may be suffering from an allergic skin reaction.

your dog has so that you'll be able to give your vet a more comprehensive evaluation of his condition.

Diarrhea

Every dog will probably have diarrhea at least once in his lifetime, and it's a sign that he is sick. It's always a good idea to observe your dog's bowel movements at least once a day to make sure that they are not loose or runny and that there are no bloody or mucus-like stools.

These abnormal bowel signs can be due to ingesting something toxic, excitement or nervousness, an abrupt change in diet or water, too much food, viral or bacterial infections, or intestinal parasites.

To treat diarrhea in your APBT, contact your veterinarian about giving your dog human antidiarrheal medication. Also, don't feed your dog his regular food for a few days. Instead, give him a bland diet consisting of cottage cheese, white rice, or broiled chicken without skin or bones.

Ear Infections

Ear infections are caused by bacteria, yeasts, or ear mites. Signs of an ear infection include redness and swelling of the ear folds in the canal, as well as a dark discharge with a bad odor. Dogs

can also have chronic ear infections caused by food allergies, other allergens, or hypothyroidism. To diagnose the infection accurately, your veterinarian can examine the ear discharge under a microscope. To treat an ear infection, your vet may clean the ear and use antibiotics.

Eye Infections

If your dog's eyes are watering or bulging or if he squints or paws at one eye, then he may have an eye infection. There are many reasons that your dog may be suffering from an eye infection.

The cornea can be irritated, or there may be a foreign body behind the upper or lower eyelid. A watery discharge may indicate an allergy, or there may be a clogged tear duct. APBTs may have juvenile cataracts, a condition in which the lens becomes cloudy. If you have any doubts about your dog's eye condition, consult a veterinary ophthalmologist. She will be able to prescribe the proper treatment for his particular condition.

Vomiting

Occasionally, dogs vomit, usually on your best rug or bedspread. While retching once in a while is fairly normal, repeated vomiting or vomiting immediately after meals can signal a serious problem. Maybe the dog has swallowed something difficult to digest, or perhaps the esophagus is obstructed. Try withholding food for a meal or two, and give your dog a bland diet instead, the same way you would for diarrhea, consisting of cottage cheese, white rice, or broiled chicken without skin or bones. Contact your veterinarian if there are repeated incidents or if your dog vomits up any blood.

Parasites

A parasite sponges off other creatures but gives nothing back in return. For dogs, parasites mean trouble. They move into their skin, intestines, bowels, and heart and generally make their lives miserable. Getting rid of parasites takes specific action, but if you discover them early enough, this can be easily accomplished through medical intervention. There are many new ways to prevent or control the most common parasites in dogs. If your dog suffers from parasites for too long, though, they are nearly impossible to banish and can be fatal.

There are two types of parasites: external and internal.

External Parasites

External parasites live on or within the skin and include fleas, ticks, lice, and mites (sarcoptic, demodex, ear, and cheyletiella). Besides being annoying, they also carry disease, and their bites can cause allergic reactions in some dogs.

Check your dog for ticks after he has been playing outside.

Fleas

There are thousands of flea species in the world, and they cause trouble wherever they go. Fleas feed on their host animals by sucking their blood. Outdoors they lay their eggs on grass, and indoors on household bedding and carpets. In allergic dogs, fleas cause dermatitis. Fortunately, with modern preventives your dog can be immune to fleabites.

Problems such as anemia and weight loss can result from internal parasite infestation.

Mites

These microscopic arachnids are responsible for several diseases:

- *Sarcoptic mange* is caused by the scabies mite and affects both puppies and young children. The female scabies mite burrows into the skin and lays eggs. They hatch into larvae, which cause lesions and secondary infections. Dogs suffering from sarcoptic mange have matted hair and crusty skin. Your veterinarian can examine the area and prescribe a medicated shampoo and an insecticide.
- *Demodex mange* mites are always present on your dog, but his immune system prevents them from doing any harm. When the immune system is weak, the mites move into the hair follicles and cause the hair to fall out. It may take several months to clear up this condition with a medicated dip.
- *Ear mites* work their way into the external ear and the ear canal. If your dog shakes his head and tries to rub his head and ears on the ground, he may have ear mites. Symptoms of ear mites include a dark discharge and odor from the ear. Your veterinarian can diagnose the problem and thoroughly clean the ear with medicated ear drops.
- *Cheyletiella,* or walking dandruff, produces hair loss, but it's not irritating to your dog. Your veterinarian can prescribe a special pesticide to clear up the condition.

Ticks

An ugly-looking parasite, ticks carry diseases that can be debilitating to both you and your dog. To look for ticks on your dog, put on a pair of thin plastic gloves. Have a small jar of alcohol and a pair of tweezers close by to help with the removal process. Working slowly, separate and move aside the hair from your dog's head, neck, chest, back, stomach, hindquarters, and legs. You can also use a fine-tooth flea comb to find ticks. If you find a tick on your APBT, wear a pair of plastic gloves when removing it. Use a pair of tweezers to carefully lift the tick's head. Pluck it out in one steady pulling motion without crushing the tick, which can spew bacteria. Once you have it, drop it down the toilet or dip it into alcohol to kill it.

Wipe the wound with some hydrogen peroxide and antibiotic ointment, and wash your hands. You may notice a welt where the tick was. If it doesn't subside within a few days, take your dog to your veterinarian, because there may be an infection.

Think back to where your dog might have picked it up. Grass and bushes in mountainous areas where other animals deposit them

are notorious tick hideouts. If your dog rubs up against a blade of grass or a bush with a tick on it, the tick will leap onto his body, looking for a blood source to feast on. Try to keep your dog away from grassy areas or bushes with ticks. If you have bushes in your yard, clip the bottom branches off so that your dog can't brush up against them. For more protection against the parasite, obtain anti-tick medication from your veterinarian.

Internal Parasites

You cannot see internal parasites, but they harm your dog from the inside out. Problems such as anemia, diarrhea, weight loss, and vomiting are actually caused by worms that are often passed from mothers to their unborn puppies during pregnancy. Your veterinarian can examine your dog's stool sample and test for the presence of these worms.

Heartworms

When infected mosquitoes bite, they pass heartworm larvae into a dog's bloodstream. Once the parasitic larvae have reached the bloodstream, they mature and reproduce into worms that clog the heart. Symptoms include coughing, breathing difficulties, and reduced energy. Preventive monthly heartworm medication is available to treat the disease.

Heartworm disease is a serious and potentially life-threatening problem that is more prevalent in some areas and virtually nonexistent in others. Check with your veterinarian to see whether you need to safeguard your dog against heartworm in your area.

Hookworms

Hookworms attach to the intestinal wall and can cause diarrhea, intestinal disease, and anemia. Your veterinarian can treat this parasite with medication that is given either orally or injected.

Ringworm

Ringworm is a fungal infection that you can recognize in a dog exhibiting circular hair loss and scaly skin. Ringworm usually disappears by itself, although an antifungal medication may be effective.

Roundworms

Roundworms are the most common internal parasites. They are usually harmless, although in affected puppies, they can be fatal. Several commercial medications are available to treat roundworms—consult your veterinarian.

Whipworms

Whipworms live in the dog's large intestine and can grow up to 3 inches (7.6 cm) long. They produce diarrhea with a strong odor and are difficult to get rid of. Whipworm eggs can survive in infected soil for several years and infect dogs who come in contact with the area. The best preventive is to pick up after your dog every day and consult with your veterinarian for advice.

Your Senior APBT

APBTs are a hardy breed, but as yours ages, be on the lookout for signs that he is getting older, such as diarrhea, coughing, eating problems (including

Feeling Good

Alternative therapies can have a positive impact on your dog's health and well-being.

decreased or increased appetite and weight loss), frequent urination, limping, and a distended abdomen. These also may be signs of illness.

Your APBT should visit the veterinarian at least twice a year for a complete blood panel. With this diagnostic procedure, your veterinarian may be able to detect the first signs of many diseases.

You have spent years caring for your dog, but there's still more that you can do to keep him healthy and active in the winter of his life. Continue brushing his teeth to remove tartar and plaque, and keep up with professional cleanings. If you notice a yellowish or

bloody eye discharge in the corner of your dog's eyes, have them checked by a veterinary ophthalmologist. Don't neglect his ears, either. Watch for cuts or scratches, as they may become infected. More important now than ever before, toenails should be kept short. Once they grow too long and begin to curl back, they can hamper your dog's ability to walk.

Alternative Therapies

When your APBT has a serious illness, you rely on your veterinarian to treat your dog and to solve the problem. Most veterinarians use traditional Western medicine, which has been tested using

Coping With a Senior's Declining Health

If only your APBT would stay young forever, but that is not destined to be. One day you will realize that your treasured pet is sleeping longer and more soundly than he once did, has difficulty walking every now and then, and is grayer around the face and muzzle than you remember. Perhaps he forgets to go outside when it's time to go to the bathroom and has trouble standing upright while he's eating.

APBTs are hardy dogs who have been known to live as long as 15 or 16 years of age, but watching your dog transition to his golden years can be sad and emotionally draining. You worry what you'll do when it's time to say good-bye to your dog and wonder when that day might come. But take heart! Enjoy every minute you have with your dog now. Make time to take him on a few short walks. Move his bed to a warmer location to help his joints feel better, or put his food bowl on a rug so that his feet don't slide. Contact your veterinarian to find out what else you can do to make your dog comfortable in his old age.

69

Feeling Good

scientific experimentation and clinical trials. Other vets will use or recommend an alternative treatment. Some alternative therapies are better than others, and it is tempting to try anything if your dog doesn't respond to traditional techniques. If you decide that an alternative therapy may be the way to go, be sure to do your research to determine which therapy is best for your dog.

Acupuncture

Acupuncture involves using thin sterilized needles to relieve pain. The needles treat muscle and skeletal abnormalities, skin disease, reproductive

What Is a Holistic Veterinarian?

A holistic practitioner looks at the whole dog—his mind, body, spirit, genetics, and environment. This is different from a traditional veterinarian, who looks at the dog's physical symptoms to decide upon a treatment.

When a holistic veterinarian treats a dog, she gives him a comprehensive physical examination and is interested in what the total picture of the dog looks like: his environment, emotional stresses, recent medical and dietary history, and behavior. The relationship of the dog with his owner and the dog's genetics and hygiene are all explored.

The holistic veterinarian develops a treatment plan using a wide range of therapies. The techniques used are gentle, minimally invasive, and incorporate well-being and stress reduction. While many traditional veterinarians incorporate alternative medicine, such as acupuncture or homeopathy, into their practice and may be truly interested in applying less harmful alternatives to routine medical treatments, they are not holistic veterinarians.

If you are looking for a truly holistic veterinarian, schedule a consultation. Expect to pay for the vet's time, but what you will learn will be well worth the expense. Ask the veterinarian what her definition of the term holistic means, how she first became involved in the practice, what her training and background are, and how long she has been practicing holistic veterinary care.

problems, and neurological illness. Inserted at specific locations beneath the skin, the needles stimulate the body to promote healing and are effective in improving athletic performance. The American Veterinarian Medical Association (AVMA) recently recognized acupuncture as a valid veterinary alternative.

Chiropractic Care

For dogs with pain in their necks, lower backs, pelvis, and knees, chiropractic treatment can be helpful. Veterinarians certified by the American Veterinary Chiropractic Association (AVCA) manipulate the spine to correct the problem. If your APBT can trust the veterinarian and relax enough while his body is being worked on, some of his pain may be alleviated.

Herbal Therapy

Botanical medicine uses plants and plant derivatives as therapeutic agents. Using these to treat disease has become popular, and many people prefer them to some of the drugs used today because they believe botanicals are safer to use for treatment than chemicals are. Actually, some botanicals contain the same amount of chemicals as traditional drugs and may be toxic if used incorrectly. Many botanicals have not been tested the way that traditional drugs have. The AVMA recommends that more research and education are needed before these substances can be called reliable.

Homeopathy

This type of treatment uses diluted amounts of extracts from plants to make them more powerful (following the belief that "less is more") so that they reproduce the symptoms of an illness. The basic idea is that symptoms of a problem are not meant to be suppressed with medication but rather used to show what the body needs to heal itself.

Homeopathic practitioners believe that this stimulates the healing process. They consider the well-being of the whole patient—mental, emotional, and physical— when deciding upon a treatment.

Massage Therapy

If you've ever enjoyed a massage, you know why your dog

would like it too. Canine sports massage therapy is the therapeutic application of hands-on deep-tissue techniques to the voluntary muscle system. It increases circulation, reduces muscle spasms, relieves tension, enhances muscle tone, and promotes healing and increased range of motion. Certified canine massage therapists are trained in canine anatomy and movement, and they know how to apply gentle pressure to specific parts of the dog's body.

Your dog depends on you to keep him healthy, but with so many advances in modern veterinary medicine today, this has never been easier. If he could speak up and tell you what bothers him every day, your job would be a cinch. Instead, you'll have to continually rely on observing your dog's behavior and physical appearance to pick up any clues about how he feels. Fortunately, the APBT is a hardy breed, who, with the proper health care, can live a long and healthy life.

Chapter 6

Being Good

Naturally independent and physically strong, APBTs are eager learners. Shaping this behavior with kindness and respect as early as possible builds your dog's self-esteem. Once he knows what the rules are and recognizes that you are in charge, he'll be much happier, because he doesn't have to experiment with new behaviors that often get him into trouble. Like a teenager who thinks she knows everything, the untrained APBT thinks he doesn't need you.

Your goal is to teach him that everything good in his life comes from you.

Why Train Your APBT?

There are many reasons for training your APBT. Besides helping you establish a rapport with your dog, teaching him what's expected of him enables you to have a canine companion who pays attention to every word you say and does exactly what he's supposed to do at all times. Well, that might be a little overstated, but having a well-trained dog makes life a lot easier.

With public opinion turning against this breed, it's important that people see that APBTs are intelligent, loving, and dependable. This is not a cute and cuddly breed that many people fall head over heels in love with right away. He doesn't have many starring movie roles these days to catch much positive light, and he isn't usually the fun

family dog you see people take along on outings.

APBTs today are carefully scrutinized and severely criticized for any signs of the slightest bad behavior. Some landlords, insurance agents, and public officials have pushed to ban this breed completely by claiming they threaten the safety of other dogs as well as humans. True, some APBTs have bitten people, but so have other breeds. The difference is that APBTs have stronger jaws than most breeds and can cause more damage.

Unless you want to see the American

Kindergarten classes for puppies are a fun way for your dog to interact with other dogs his age.

74

Pit Bull Terrier banned everywhere, take the time that's necessary to make sure your dog is properly trained.

Socialization

Socialization is the process of helping your dog become comfortable with the sights, sounds, and other experiences of everyday life. The best way to raise a well-adjusted APBT is to socialize, socialize, socialize. This means taking your puppy out of the house as soon as your veterinarian tells you it's okay—sometime between 7 and 14 weeks of age. Try to give your puppy as many new experiences as you can so that he'll be confident, rather than fearful, of new people and experiences as he grows.

By the time your puppy is 16 weeks old, he should meet 100 people, from babies to seniors, and objects like a stroller, the garbage truck, cameras, and odd, scary noises to build his confidence.

Kindergarten classes for puppies three to five months old are a fun way for your dog to interact with other dogs his same age. This course is the foundation of everything your dog will ever do, from formal dog sports to belonging to the Good Dog Club in your own household.

If you acquire an older APBT, he already has opinions about children,

The Expert Knows

Finding a Trainer

The right dog trainer can mean the difference between having a dependable, well-behaved APBT and an unpredictable pet. To find a qualified, reputable trainer, ask your veterinarian, breeder, or rescue coordinator for the names of people they recommend. When interviewing trainers, ask them if they've owned or trained APBTs. The trainer should have experience with the breed. Inquire about what their training methods are. A good trainer won't be locked into any one method or tool and is never abusive or cruel.

adults, other dogs, and noises. Don't assume that just because your older dog is fearful that he's been abused. He's probably never been out of his prior home or kennel and hasn't experienced much. Fortunately, it's not too late to socialize him. You just have to spend more time doing it.

If your older APBT has been trained as a fighting dog, you probably have a lot of retraining to do. Don't hesitate to call a professional trainer.

Crate Training

A crate is not a jail or a place to punish your dog. Think of it as a doggy

Yummy Rewards

To make training exciting and to motivate your dog to do his best, use food rewards that he doesn't normally receive. Offer new and different food treats from time to time, too. This way, your APBT will work a little harder to complete a task, because he never knows what he will receive.

Avoid big, hard, and crunchy treat pieces, because they take too much time for your dog to eat. Cut them into bite-size chunks. Use soft but firm treats, and put them into a waist pack or a big pocket so that you can dole them out quickly. Human food is the most enticing for dogs, but make it healthy! Small pieces of hot dogs, cooked chicken, roast beef, turkey, string cheese, apples, or carrots work wonders.

playpen. When you can't watch your APBT or when you're trying to housetrain your dog, putting him inside the crate will reassure you that he's not destroying the house. In addition, it gives him a place to call his own.

How to Crate Train Your APBT

Begin training your dog to like being inside his crate by putting it in a room where you or the family spends the most time. Don't put it in a place where your dog can't see you, because he'll only cry for your attention. If you know your puppy or dog won't chew up a comfy blanket, put one on the crate bottom with some safe toys. It helps to place him inside when he's already tired so he learns that this is his special bed.

Every time you want your dog to go into the crate, make sure that he sees you throw a treat inside. When he follows the treat, close the door. Say, "Good boy!" and after a few seconds, let him out. Repeat this process, and gradually lengthen the amount of time he's in there. Slowly build up to leaving him there and walking out of the room for five minutes, adding time as he becomes more comfortable.

If your dog is really fearful of going inside the crate, try feeding him his meals inside. He'll soon associate having a positive experience with the crate.

Housetraining

Training your APBT to go to the bathroom outdoors instead of inside the house isn't as hard as it sounds. APBTs will housetrain quickly, as long as you're committed to supervising your puppy 24/7. This includes staying outside with him until he relieves himself.

How to Housetrain Your APBT

Here's where crate training comes in handy. Dogs generally will not urinate or defecate where they sleep. Thus, you can use the crate to set up a schedule so that you'll know when your APBT needs to go to the bathroom. Count on first thing in the morning when he comes out of the crate. Take him to the same spot outdoors, and stay there with him until he relieves himself. Tell him, "Good dog," and bring him inside for his breakfast.

Immediately after the morning meal, take him outside to the same spot he used earlier. Once he's finished and comes inside, use baby gates to restrict his

freedom to one or two rooms so that you can easily keep an eye on him. He'll be ready to go to the bathroom again 20 to 30 minutes later, so if you see him sniffing the floor or turning in circles, it's a sign he's ready. It may take you a few days to become accustomed to this schedule, but if you're diligent about taking your dog out at the right times, housetraining shouldn't take longer than about a month.

If Your APBT Has an Accident

If your APBT has an accident, he's likely to return to that spot again if you let him, so clean it with some antibacterial spray and block it off. Where your dog is concerned, completely ignore the mishap. If you see your dog going to the bathroom inside the house say, "No," and quickly take him outside, even in midstream. Rubbing his nose in the mess, hitting him with a newspaper or your hand, or yelling and screaming at him doesn't work and will only make him think that the urge to go to the bathroom means he'll be punished.

Taking your APBT outside on a regular schedule will help him become housetrained faster.

Reading Your APBT's Body Language

Even without speaking, your APBT is trying to communicate with you. Dogs use more than 100 different body positions and facial expressions to say what they are thinking. For example, observe if your dog's tail is high or low, and you'll have an idea about whether your dog is feeling like he's in charge or not. High wagging shows dominance, while fast, down wagging signals submission. Also, when a dog crouches down with his rear in the air, he wants to play. Leaning forward signals guarding behavior. A soft gaze means that a dog trusts you, while a direct stare at your face shows interest in what you're doing and possibly indicates a challenge.

Once you learn to read your dog's body language, training your APBT will become much easier.

Basic Obedience Commands

Although training makes perfect sense to you, convincing your APBT that this is a good idea can be a challenge, especially if you've never trained a dog before. It's not a question of whether or not your APBT is smart enough to learn basic skills; it's a matter of how willing he is to please you. Your job is to motivate him to listen to everything you tell him to do.

All APBTs, no matter how old they are or where they came from, can learn the basic obedience commands. It just takes time, patience, and a lot of tasty treats. While some dogs will definitely work for food, others don't respond to that at all. This means you'll have to use whatever excites your dog, whether it is a ball, flying disk, furry toy, or hard plastic bone.

Limit each training session to five or ten minutes. Feel free to add extra sessions throughout the day. This keeps training fun and spontaneous. If you become frustrated, stop training, because your dog won't learn anything if you're angry.

Watch Me

Teaching your APBT how to pay attention to you, no matter what you tell him, is the foundation of all training. Regardless of how old your APBT is when you bring him home, introduce the *watch me* command to him right away.

How to Teach Watch Me

Find a nice, quiet place inside your home away from any distractions for training. Then, with your dog in front of you, say, "Watch me." As soon as your dog looks at you, quickly give him a treat. Repeat this a few times over several sessions, and gradually wait a little longer each time before rewarding. When you think your dog knows how to look at you until you release him, take him outdoors where there are distractions to reinforce the learning.

Sit

When your dog is in the *sit* position, it's easy to control him, especially if he wants to do something you don't want him to do, such as jumping at the door

when someone enters your home or running out the front door when it opens.

How to Teach Sit

To teach the *sit* command, stand in front of your APBT and show him a treat. Hold it slightly above his head in front of his eyes. Say, "Sit," and bring your hand above his eyes. Your dog will look at the treat and back up into a sitting position. When he sits, give him the treat before he has a chance to stand up. Using an upbeat, happy voice, tell him, "Good boy!"

What should you do if your dog doesn't sit? Say, "Sit," gently put your left hand under his tail behind his knees and your right hand against his chest, and slowly guide him into a sitting position. Don't push, because your dog will only resist. When he sits, tell him, "Good boy!" If someone can give him a treat at the same time, he'll

Being Good

It's easy to control your dog when he is in the sit *position.*

FAMILY-FRIENDLY TIP

How to Involve Your Child in Training

Like peanut butter and jelly, there's a magical combination between most children and puppies. Studies have shown that caring for a dog helps children develop good nurturing skills. To keep this relationship going, make dog training with your child a fun experience, and always supervise your child and dog's activities.

Adults should always teach the dog any new behaviors, while children should give commands for skills the dog already knows. Don't expect your dog to listen to your child as he does to you. When it comes to giving commands, children tend to say them too many times, so dogs tune them out.

When involving your child with training, say the command that you'd like your dog to follow, and assist your child with handling the treat. Many children have trouble holding and releasing the treat at the right time, because they're afraid the dog will grab their hand. Instead, give your child a bowl in which to put the treat and extend the bowl to the dog, or teach your child to drop the treat on the floor or toss it to your APBT. To assist you with crate training, your child can call the dog and toss the treat inside the crate.

have an extra reward in addition to your praise.

Some dogs learn to sit right away, and others take longer. Never fear. All APBTs, no matter how old they are, can learn to sit.

Stay

Once your dog is in a sitting position, you'll want him to remain there for a few minutes. The *stay* command lets your dog know that he needs to keep doing what you have already asked him to do.

How to Teach Stay

Once your APBT knows how to sit, teaching him to stay is easy. In the beginning, your dog should remain, or stay, in the *sit* position for just a few seconds; you can eventually build up to five minutes. After he sits, give him the cue to stay until you tell him, "Okay!"

Say, "Stay!" and take a few steps away from him. If he remains in place, give him a treat. Don't give him anything if he gets up. Instead, gently put him back in the *sit*.

Teaching the *stand stay* is the same process, except that you will begin with your dog in the standing position.

Come

Once your dog learns to respond to the *come* command, you can depend on him to return to you if you're both outdoors. For example, if he's running toward a car, your request to come to you may save his life.

How to Teach Come

To teach *come,* begin by putting your dog's leash on. Tell your dog, "Stand, stay!" With the leash in your right hand, face your dog and slowly take a few steps backward, saying, "Come!" When he follows you, keep walking backward. After a few steps, stop and say, "Come!" As your APBT comes toward you, praise him and give him a treat. Repeat a few times.

Down

The *down* command can save your dog's life. If he's loose and you don't want him going any farther, telling him to down enables him to stop in his tracks without trying to get back to you and possibly getting hit by an oncoming vehicle. This cue also comes in handy if your dog needs to remain in one place for longer than five minutes.

How to Teach Down

With your dog in a sitting position facing you, take

The down *command enables your dog to stop in his tracks, potentially keeping him out of harm's way.*

a piece of food and lower it to the floor away from your dog's nose. Don't let him get up. If he does, go back to the *sit* position. As he begins to lie down to follow the food say, "Down!" When his body touches the floor, give him the treat.

Heel (Walk Nicely on a Leash)

Teaching a puppy how to walk on a leash without pulling you is so much easier than trying to teach a full-grown dog. It may take your dog several sessions to learn, but you'll definitely appreciate it when you take your powerful APBT for a walk.

How to Teach Heel

To teach *heel,* keep your dog on your left side, and hold the leash in your right hand. Start walking and say your dog's name, followed by the command, "Heel!" If he lunges forward, turn around quickly and go the other way. Repeat this step several times, choosing

SENIOR DOG TIP

Training Techniques for the Older Dog

Yes, you can teach an old dog new tricks. You just need to have a little more patience and a lot more treats. Older dogs aren't as alert as they once were, so give commands loudly and repeat them a few extra times. If your dog has trouble standing, train on a nonslick surface to prevent sliding. Always use positive training with your oldster, and never punish him if he doesn't do what you want him to do. As dogs age, they are more willing to please you than when they were younger, but it takes them longer to learn new concepts.

different directions. When he walks without pulling you, praise him with a treat and some words of praise.

Tricks

Teaching your dog obedience is necessary and serious stuff, but learning tricks is just plain fun. Watching your dog figure out how to raise one paw and give you a "high five" is a guaranteed good time. Besides

the laughs, learning a few tricks gives your dog another opportunity to exercise his magnificent brain.

What tricks can you teach an APBT? APBTs are capable of learning anything you teach them. All it takes is patience, consistency, and reinforcement.

Before getting started, make sure you have plenty of really good food treats for rewards. Set aside five to ten minutes of uninterrupted time for each training session. It's better to have shorter, more frequent sessions, rather than just a few long ones. Your dog will enjoy it more and won't get bored. For the initial training, choose an area of your home to work in that's fairly quiet and not distracting. As your dog begins to master the behaviors, you can add distractions to test his learning.

The best way to teach tricks is to break the behaviors down into small parts so that your dog can learn each one, which leads to the final act.

The following are some simple tricks that you can teach your dog.

Catch

Say your dog's name, followed by the command *catch*. Toss a small piece of food toward your dog's face. If he doesn't catch it, pick it up quickly before he gets it. Repeat a few times, but don't give your dog any freebie treats. Soon he'll realize that he'll have to grab it before you do. Don't teach this trick if your dog is possessive about his food.

When your dog can walk nicely on leash without pulling you, praise and treat him.

Shake Hands

Have your dog sit. Extend your palm toward him at your chest level, and say his name and the word "shake." Lift his elbow a few inches (cm), and slide your hand down to the paw and gently shake it. Verbally praise him by saying, "Good boy!" Give him a food reward and release the paw. Repeat this a few times over several sessions.

The Other One

To teach your dog to give you his other paw, tell him, "Shake." When he lifts his paw, tell him, "The other one."

Point to the other leg. As soon as he lifts the other paw, give him a treat and verbally praise him. With practice, your dog will offer one paw after the other.

Training your APBT takes time and patience, but the effort is well worth it. Your dog needs to be well behaved and under control at all times. You want people to respect and admire your dog, and nothing gets the message across faster than seeing an intelligent companion who knows how to follow the rules.

Chapter 7

In the
Doghouse

No one likes a juvenile APBT delinquent. You expect your dog to behave and to follow household rules, but when it looks like he's forgotten everything he's learned, you might get frustrated.

This is an active, curious breed with lots of stamina, so it doesn't take much for an APBT to develop some bad habits.

When your dog jumps up on you and plants paw prints on your clothing, or you have to clean up a bathroom accident in the house, it's irritating. So is his incessant barking, especially if you have neighbors who complain about the noise. Then there's digging up the yard. Maybe you wouldn't mind one hole in your manicured lawn, but when your APBT excavates a tunnel beneath the fence and runs away, it's upsetting. Chewing is downright destructive, and with such strong jaws, when an APBT nips, it can be dangerous.

So what can you do about these problem behaviors? You may decide that it's easier to live with them rather than try to fix them. After all, it takes time, energy, and patience to transform your APBT into a good household citizen. But you should never tolerate any behavior that threatens the safety of you,

The APBT is an active, curious dog with a great deal of stamina.

your dog, or others. This is part of the responsibility of owning a dog.

To begin solving a problem behavior, you should consider that your dog may be acting out due to a variety of reasons, including boredom, not enough exercise, insufficient quality time with you, loneliness, or nutrition or health problems. When dogs are left alone at home for long hours during the day, there may be nothing for them to do except to find trouble. To break up your dog's daily grind, take him to doggy day care one or more times a week, or hire a dog walker to exercise your dog.

APBTs need plenty of exercise. A tired APBT is a happy dog, but you don't have to

Finding a Behaviorist

If you've already taken your dog through an obedience class or hired a private trainer to come to your home, but your dog still needs more attention, a behaviorist may be able to help you. To find a veterinary behaviorist, ask your veterinarian for a recommendation, or contact the American Veterinary Medical Association (AVMA). These professionals are certified by the American College of Veterinary Behaviorists (ACVB) and are usually located at veterinary colleges in large cities. A veterinary behaviorist uses behavior modification and prescription medication, if necessary, to help solve a problem.

run a marathon with your dog to prevent deviant behavior. A walk every day, chasing the ball down the hallway, or running up and down stairs to retrieve a toy are healthy alternatives.

There are usually reasons that your dog isn't doing what you want him to. He's not being stubborn, self-centered, or mean. He's being a dog who needs to feel useful and mentally and physically stimulated.

Always remember that if your dog continues to misbehave, despite your behavioral-modification techniques, you should contact your veterinarian. Your dog may need professional attention to deal with his behavioral issues.

Barking

Dogs speak volumes by barking. It's their natural way to communicate, and they use their vocal chords to say everything. If your dog barks at the right times and stops when you ask him to, then barking is not a problem. When he barks too often and can't seem to calm

himself down once he gets started, though, it's your job to convince him to stop. No one likes all that canine noise disturbing the neighborhood, and the last thing you want is someone complaining to animal control officials about an out-of-control APBT.

Solution

There's no sense in barking if your dog doesn't really have something meaningful to say. If a stranger comes to your door and your APBT barks to alert you, that's appropriate barking. To get him to stop once he's begun, simply acknowledge him by saying, "That's enough."

If, on the other hand, your dog goes out to the yard and always barks 20 minutes later at nothing you can see, figure out his motivation for barking and how you can stop him from doing it. Most likely, he's feeling anxious, bored, or lonely. When there's the briefest minute that he's quiet, bring him indoors. That way, you're not rewarding

How to Train Older Dogs out of Entrenched Problem Behaviors

It's a scientific fact that dogs can learn new behaviors, no matter how old they are. To teach them some new tricks, accept the notion that the only thing dogs really want is the good stuff. Your job is to convince them that what you want them to do earns the prize. Unwanted behavior wins them nothing.

Here's how to do it: Know what behavior you want to teach, don't reinforce the behavior you're trying to fix, and generously reward your dog for doing what he's supposed to do. Remember to be consistent and patient. This method may take a little longer to get the message across, but it's kind and gentle. Physical punishment doesn't work in the long run, and besides hurting your dog when it's not necessary, this type of reinforcement only builds resentment and aggression in your dog.

him for barking. The next time you let him outside, don't leave him out for longer than 15 minutes. Also, try putting

him outside with different toys so that he's not bored, or stay outdoors with him for a while and play with him.

Your APBT may be barking at people passing by the yard. He could feel possessive about the yard and want to protect it. Meanwhile, the noise is irritating, and neighbors might not appreciate constant barking all day and night. If possible, close all the curtains so that your dog can't see out. If he can't see what's going on outside, he's less likely to bark.

Chewing

Virtually all puppies have a physiological need to chew while they're teething. Their gums are sore, and they look for things to soothe the discomfort. With his strong jaws, an APBT puppy can be a vigorous chomper, and nothing is safe in your home.

Solution

To protect your valuable items, put them out of your dog's reach, and keep an eye on him at all times. To prevent your dog from gnawing his way through your furniture, shoes, clothing, and carpeting, provide him with safe toys he can chew.

Your pet supply store has a wide range of safe toys your dog can dig his teeth into, such as ropes, sturdy canvas, and tough rubber toys. Hard dog biscuits, apples, and carrots will also keep his jaws busy.

By the time your dog is two years

Barking is a dog's natural way of communicating.

old, his adult teeth and molars will have come in, and the primary urge to chew will disappear. An older APBT who is still chewing is bored, anxious, or lonely, so every effort should be made to increase his exercise and give him more quality time.

There will be occasions when you won't be able to watch your APBT. When that happens, use baby gates or close doors to rooms you don't want your dog to wander into. You can also give him some chew toys and put him into an exercise pen or his crate.

Digging

Besides the mess and destruction to your garden, digging is a major problem if your dog is an escape artist and tries to dig his way out of the yard. Fortunately, there are a few things you can do to manage the holes and flying dirt.

Solution

To prevent digging from occurring near the perimeter of your yard, first make some changes in your yard to hamper your APBT's fascination with earth moving. One solution is to fence off an inner portion of the yard so that your dog can't reach the gate or perimeter wall to dig out. Or if the fence line he's digging under isn't too long, put large, heavy bricks up against the fence, or pour concrete a few feet underneath the fence line.

In other parts of the yard, your dog may be digging because he wants to

Lost and Found

To protect your APBT in case you become separated from him, make sure that his collar fits snugly and has a legible identification tag firmly attached to it. Your name, current address, and telephone number (including your correct area code) should be on the tag. This gives the person who finds your dog a way to locate you. For extra protection, have your dog microchipped.

If your dog becomes lost, start looking for him right away. Don't wait, and don't assume that your dog will find his way back to you. Even people can lose their sense of direction once they leave home. Dogs are no different. The chances of finding him are much greater the sooner you begin your search. Put up large posters with a picture of your dog everywhere you can think of: the shelter, police station, schools, veterinary clinics, and nearby businesses. Visit local animal shelters, and contact local APBT breeders or rescue organizations to alert them of your loss. Stay close to the location where he was last seen. Offer a large reward. Hopefully, this will deter someone who finds your dog from deciding to keep him for fighting.

see what's there, because the earth is cool on a warm day, because it's fun, because he's burying or digging up a bone, or because he's bored or frustrated. In these cases, the one sure way to prevent your dog from digging is to watch him constantly, but this may not be practical. An alternative is to try to deter him from doing this dirty deed.

Training your dog not to dig is next to impossible, but you can encourage your dog to dig in a certain spot. Create a designated digging area for your dog by putting a small fence around it and hiding some of your dog's toys beneath the dirt. Take him to this spot and tell him, "Dig." When he digs, tell him he's a good dog. Keep taking him there, and soon he'll go there on his own.

If there are landscaped areas you absolutely don't want him excavating, fence them off. Check building supply warehouses for interior fencing products. The best deterrent to digging is to make sure your APBT has plenty of exercise. A tired dog is not necessarily a digging dog. Frequently rotating his toys helps, too. With any luck, he'll eventually lose interest in digging.

Housesoiling

You thought your APBT was housetrained, but now he's having soiling accidents in the house. Why now? There are several reasons for this, as well as several solutions.

Solution

If something new or different is happening in the household, such as visiting guests, your dog may be stressed out. This, in turn, may cause him to eliminate in the house. If this is the case, make a point of spending special time with your dog, and take him outdoors more often.

Perhaps you've left your dog too long without giving him a chance to go to the bathroom. To fix this problem, let him out when he needs to go out so that eliminating in the house doesn't become a habit. Don't make him wait too long.

Another explanation for housesoiling is that maybe your APBT has eaten something that doesn't agree with him, or if you have a female, she could have a bladder infection, which causes frequent urination. Senior dogs can be incontinent, too. Other than taking your APBT outdoors more frequently, there may be nothing you can do to prevent your older dog from having household accidents. Somehow, knowing that aging is the reason can make you feel better about your old companion.

If your dog continues to soil in the house, contact your veterinarian.

Digging can be a major problem if your dog is trying to dig his way out of the yard.

If you want to stop your APBT from jumping up to greet you, teach him to welcome you with a sit instead.

Jumping Up

When your APBT was a puppy, it was cute when he stretched and popped up his paws on your legs

FAMILY-FRIENDLY TIP

Children and APBT Safety

Children and dogs don't always take to one another easily, and both must be taught to understand and respect the other. One misunderstanding can be dangerous, as millions of children who have been bitten by various breeds each year will tell you. As a parent, it is your responsibility to protect your child from your APBT and vice versa.

The APBT is a strong breed that needs to be supervised around children at all times. Establishing rules, supervising their interaction, controlling the environment, and teaching your child from a young age the do's and don'ts of how to care for your dog will go a long way toward preventing accidents.

over, he's left mud stripes on your pants and shirt. Dogs don't intend to dirty your clothes when they jump up on you, but it happens. This is just their way to greet you, but this warm welcome can be dangerous. When APBTs propel themselves toward you, they don't realize their own strength and that they can throw you off balance.

Solution

If you want to stop your APBT from giving you an airborne welcome, teach him to greet you with a *sit* instead. He can't launch himself at you if he's sitting.

Another way to get the message across is not to give him any attention or any opportunities to jump. When you see him running toward you, turn and take a step away so that he can't jump on you from any angle. Continue turning and stepping until he waits or sits. When he pauses, give him a treat to lure him into a sitting position. Give him several rewards when he continues sitting. If he lunges again, turn and step away, and repeat the process. It may take awhile, but eventually he'll figure out that you won't return his affection when he pounces.

To make this a permanent change, you must be consistent. If you give in just once and pet your dog when he jumps up, he'll try it again next time. Pushing him down doesn't help, either. He's still getting your attention.

to greet you. Who can resist petting a puppy when he goes to that much trouble? Your dog quickly learned that if he jumped up on you, you would pet him.

Fast-forward to now, when your dog is full-grown and he takes a flying leap at you just to say, "Hi!" Now it's not so cute. If he didn't knock you

Aggression: When to Seek Professional Help

If, for any reason, you think you need assistance from a dog professional, don't hesitate to contact one. Don't be lulled into a false sense of security by thinking that your puppy or young dog is sweet most of the time but acts up on occasion. Aggressive tendencies can show up or escalate when an APBT is 18 months to 2 years old.

The best time to call for help is before your dog bites someone. Watch your dog's body language and his face for signs of aggression before it's too late. Do his eyes have a fixed, frozen stare? Are his lips curling? Is he growling or snapping? If your dog does any of these things, exhibits general obnoxious or aggressive behavior, or mouths your arm or leg and punctures the skin, it's time to call a qualified professional trainer or behaviorist who has experience retraining aggressive dogs. These incidents are the beginning stages of bite aggression, and they may be resolved with qualified behavior-modification training.

Some people think that stepping on a dog's back feet or pinching his front paws when he hops up will teach him to stop, but that's painful and cruel and doesn't work. Touching him in any way leads him to think that you are returning his greeting.

Nipping

APBT puppies explore the world with their mouths, and that exploration includes soft human flesh.

Solution

By the time puppies are six months old, they need to know that mouthing human hands isn't acceptable behavior. If your puppy nips your hands, offer him an acceptable toy instead. When he reaches for your hands, yell, "Ouch," and move out of the way.

If he passes up a chance to nip, reward him with a food treat or by saying, "Good boy!" and continue playing with him.

If you continue having a problem with nipping, consult a qualified trainer, but don't wait too long. A nip can easily turn into a bite.

All of these problem behaviors are fixable, but before your APBT can become the ideal companion you want him to be, you'll need to spend the time and energy it takes to get the job done. Believe that your dog is fully capable of learning what you want him to do, and don't give up. Training your APBT well is the best way you can show him your love and devotion.

In the Doghouse

Chapter 8

Stepping Out

Your APBT is more than just a pretty face. He's an active, intelligent, and athletic dog who likes to get out every now and then and have a good time, just like you do. Besides going for a walk or a jog around the block, APBTs enjoy a wide range of activities and are willing to please you. They will like what you like. On the other hand, APBTs who are kept confined all the time in the house or backyard are quickly bored and may become overly protective.

To have the happy, personable dog that APBTs are meant to be, start taking your dog out when he's a puppy or as soon as you acquire him. Provide as much training as you possibly can right away, and he'll quickly learn that the world is a fun, friendly place. All that training will come in handy when you want to travel with your APBT or become involved in dog sports.

Travel and Vacationing

Getting away from it all with your APBT can be a lot of fun, but don't count on having the trip of your dreams. Dogs aren't allowed in most public places, especially restaurants, and unless you're going camping or spending your vacation in a dog-friendly resort, your dog will be spending a lot of time riding in the car in his crate or on a leash all the time at rest stops.

If the weather is warm, don't ever leave your APBT alone in a parked car, even for a few minutes. He can become overheated, go into convulsions, and die.

Traveling with your dog on a plane? If so, the airlines have strict rules about transporting dogs, and a few airlines don't accept APBTs. Before leaving, contact the airlines to find out what their restrictions are.

Still want to hit the road with your APBT? If so, there are some precautions you can take to make sure that you and your dog have a safe, happy trip. When

Travel Essentials

- bottled water or water from home
- carpet cleaner (in case your dog has an accident in the hotel room)
- chew toys
- close-fitting collar with identification tag
- crate
- dog bed
- dog food
- doggy seat belt harness
- exercise pen (if traveling by car)
- first-aid kit for your dog (include anti-diarrhea and allergy medication)
- food and water bowls or paper disposable bowls
- leash (short and long)
- plastic bags (for waste cleanup)
- prescription medication
- sheets (to put over the bedspread)
- towels (for cleaning your dog)
- treats
- waterless shampoo (in case your dog gets dirty)

he's riding in the car (the back seat is safer than the front), put a special travel harness on him. This attaches to the seat belt. Or put him inside a crate and make sure that it is anchored down so that it won't go flying in case there's an accident. Include your name, address, and telephone number on the outside of the crate, as well as the name and phone number of a family member or a close friend for another emergency contact.

Pack along your dog's food and plenty of bottled water for him to drink.

Every water supply has different minerals, which can upset your dog's gastrointestinal tract and cause diarrhea.

Once you arrive at your lodging destination, ask the desk clerk if there's a designated dog-walking area you should use. Be sure to take your dog there and pick up and dispose of any mess properly. Want to hang out in your room with your dog on the bed? If so, bring along a sheet from home to cover the room's bedspread. That way, if your dog sheds a little or happens to drool, you won't have to pay to have the bedspread cleaned.

Your dog should always be on a leash, too. If you have room to bring an exercise pen with you, you can sit outdoors with your dog and not have to keep his leash on. But be sure to supervise him at all times, and don't leave him unattended while he's in the pen.

Don't leave your dog alone in your room, either. He may feel abandoned in a strange place and bark and disturb the other guests. If you and your dog are responsible

Never leave your APBT alone in a parked car.

97

FAMILY-FRIENDLY TIP

Traveling With Your Dog and Child

Leaving home can be exciting and traumatic for children and dogs. To make the journey a pleasant one for everyone, plan ahead. Make sure that you have reservations for lodging that accepts children and dogs. If it has a play area and a designated dog-walking area, that's a bonus. When you're calling for accommodations, be sure and ask if the establishment is APBT friendly. There are some areas of the country that have legislation prohibiting APBTs or require them to be neutered and wearing a muzzle while in public. Know the restrictions where you are going before you leave home so that you won't be surprised.

Although you don't want to pack too much stuff, taking the right comforts from home can make traveling less stressful and more fun. Don't forget to pack food, bottled water, toys, and favorite pillows for both your child and your APBT. Keep the travel schedule somewhat flexible and at a slower pace to allow for plenty of time for rest stops, naps, and mealtimes.

One word of caution—keep your eyes on your child and your dog at all times. You don't want other children or strangers with other dogs coming up to your APBT to play when you're not looking. Adolescent APBTs between the ages of 9 and 14 months may suddenly want to prove to new dogs how strong they are and may decide to take them on. You need to be aware of your dog's possible confrontational behavior and be ready to redirect your dog's attention. Training your dog before you take him away with you will teach him to ignore other canines.

guests, the hotel or motel will continue to allow future guests to check in with their dogs.

Therapy Work

If you enjoy visiting patients at hospitals and rehabilitation centers and seniors at assisted living centers, consider training your APBT to become a therapy dog. The breed never runs out of love to dispense, and there are several organizations in your community that may welcome well-behaved, good-natured APBTs into their programs. With his confidence and high tolerance for pain, APBTs are popular canine visitors. They love to entertain by performing tricks and demonstrating their obedience training, and they are tolerant of walkers, wheelchairs, and accidental rough petting.

Canine Good Citizen

Once your APBT knows the basic obedience exercises, it doesn't hurt to give him a final exam. The American Kennel Club's (AKC's) Canine Good Citizen (CGC) program offers a CGC certificate for dogs who can master certain aspects of good behavior and handle situations that they may encounter in real life.

To prep your dog to earn a CGC certificate, contact the AKC to learn what's required. Many obedience classes provide supplemental CGC training for dogs and their owners, but with only a small amount of training that you can do at home, your APBT can pass the test. Any extra training that you can give your APBT will help him become a better companion.

When your dog earns the CGC certificate, it shows that he has good manners and behaves in public. This may come in handy if you have to convince your insurance company, landlord, or city official that your dog is well behaved and under your control.

Show dogs should have certain characteristics that match the breed standard as closely as possible.

SENIOR DOG TIP

Tips on Traveling With Older Dogs

Senior APBTs are accustomed to their daily routines, but when it's time to hop into the car, they're up for anything. If, on the other hand, your dog has never traveled before, taking him out for a long car ride now that he's older may be a little traumatic and physically difficult for him. His eyesight may be failing, he may be getting incontinent, or his joints may be stiff or sore. Consider the fact that your dog may be more comfortable staying at home with a pet sitter.

If you decide to take your dog with you, and you're traveling by car, buckle your dog into a dog seat belt to keep him safe, or insist that he ride in his crate. Even though your senior may have ridden in your car for years, he still needs to be safe on the highway.

Plan to stop every three hours so that your dog can relieve himself, and be sure to clean up after him. Also, bring along his familiar bedding from home so that he has something familiar to snuggle into.

100

Showing Your APBT

Chances are you've seen a dog show on television and may wonder if your APBT could be a show dog and earn a championship title. It's possible if your dog is from a show-bred litter. The dogs' parents should be United Kennel Club (UKC)–registered APBTs.

Show dogs need to have certain characteristics that match a description, called a breed standard, of what the breed should look and act like. At a dog show, a judge evaluates each dog to see how closely he conforms to the breed standard and compares him to other dogs who are entered at the same show. Males are evaluated separately from females, and one male and one female is chosen. The winners receive points, which accumulate from show to show until enough are accumulated to earn a championship title. Once dogs have earned their titles, they can continue competing.

Since dog shows were originally created to choose breeding stock, appearance and attitude is nearly everything. A champion APBT should look and act just like his ancestors did, having the tenacity of the terrier and the strength and athleticism of the Bulldog.

To find out more about dog shows, visit a few, but don't bring your APBT just yet. Dogs must be entered in the show ahead of time.

APBTs can compete at shows sponsored by the American Dog

Breeders Association and the UKC. There are shows several times a month throughout the United States and other countries, and you can talk with show breeders to find out more. Showing your dog is a fun way to bond with your dog. You'll do a lot of training and traveling, but you will also meet other APBT lovers and pick up tips about ABPT behavior, care, and health.

Sports

If you think you'd like to do more with your dog than hanging out at home, consider getting involved in dog sports. You'll be attending regular training classes, practicing between classes, and spending a lot of quality time with your dog. Besides getting out and having fun, you'll be strengthening the bond with your dog and directing some of his energy.

Participating in sports and activities with your APBT will strengthen your bond.

Competitive Obedience

Once your APBT has had basic obedience training, he can enter obedience competitions with the UKC.

Besides having something fun to do with your dog in your spare time, participating in this sport is something that your dog will remember and can use for the rest of his life, both at home and out in public. In competitive obedience, dogs must perform basic exercises, such as walk on a leash beside his owner without pulling, sit, stay, come, lie down, and stand for an examination.

UKC obedience competition has three levels and offers three

titles: U-CD, U-CDX, and U-UD. Once a dog has a CD title, he can enter Intermediate (CDX) competition and progress to Advanced (UD), which is the most difficult level. When your APBT has mastered these formal techniques, he's ready to compete in other dog sports.

Schutzhund Trials

Contrary to what some people think, Schutzhund trials are not designed to train dogs to attack humans. Originally created just for German Shepherd Dogs to determine quality dogs for breeding in Germany, other breeds now participate in Schutzhund.

In Schutzhund, the dog is under the owner's control and is tested on the ability to follow directions, similar to obedience and agility. In this event, dogs use their teeth to grasp a heavily padded sleeve worn by an individual. Because of the potential danger involved, this sport shouldn't be done casually. If you're interested, have your

dog evaluated first by a professional trainer.

There are three phases of Schutzhund: tracking, obedience, and protection. Dogs can progress through three levels—novice, intermediate, and advanced—with each level becoming more difficult.

Weight Pulling

APBTs know how to pull their weight, and to prove it, they can compete in weight-pulling competitions sponsored by ADBA and the International Weight Pull Association (IWPA). There is some training involved, however, which is challenging if your dog is already obedience trained and has been taught not to pull on the leash.

Wearing a custom-fitted harness, male and female APBTs compete within their weight ranges. In ADBA competition, dogs pull a cart and weight for a distance of 15 feet (4.6 m) in 60 seconds and earn a weight-pulling title called an "Ace." IWPA requires dogs to pull the weight 16 feet (4.9 m) in 60 seconds and awards a Working Dog (WD) title. There are advanced title levels in both organizations.

Games

The following games are a fun way to bond with your APBT while participating in some outdoor sports that you can both enjoy.

Hiking

Ready for an outdoor adventure with your APBT? If so, hiking may be right up your trail. Many people have discovered how much fun it is to take a hike with their dogs. Whether you're up for an hour's walk or a longer hike, your APBT will love communing with nature. But before you head for the hills, you'll need to know a few things:

1. Not all trails allow dogs, so find out where dogs are permitted before you leave home. Hike only where dogs are allowed.
2. All nature areas require dogs to be on a leash at all times.
3. Make sure that your dog's collar fits snugly and won't fall off. His identification tag should be up to date and easy to read.
4. Carry water for your dog—8

To have the happy, person-able dog that your APBT is meant to be, start taking him out when he's a puppy.

ounces (236.6 ml) for every hour of hiking is recommended.

5. If he's going to wear a pack, make sure it fits securely and doesn't interfere with his walking.

6. Take along waste cleanup bags and dispose of them properly.

7. Bring along a canine first-aid kit that includes veterinary bandage wraps, gauze pads, an antihistamine, disinfectant cream, tweezers and petroleum jelly to cover ticks, a cell phone, and your veterinarian's phone number.

8. Introduce hiking to your dog gradually with short hour-long hikes before attempting longer ones.

Outdoor sports are a perfect fit for the athletic APBT.

9. During winter hikes, protect your dog's feet with dog booties.

10. Stay on the hiking trail at all times.

Retrieving

Teaching your APBT to retrieve is a fun way to help him channel his energy. Gather several of his toys and toss one of them. Tell him, "Go get it!" When he runs after it and brings it back, praise him. Don't grab it out of his mouth or play tug-of-war with him. APBTs are too strong to wrestle with, and you don't want him thinking he can win. If he doesn't drop the toy, throw another toy, and when he drops the first one, pick it up and say, "Good dog!"

If your dog is too busy running

around with the first toy to drop it, then simply stop playing and leave the area. It's best not to chase after him or tease him into dropping it. Try the game again later. You may have to start and stop playing several times until he understands what you want, but eventually he'll get the picture.

One of the best reasons to have a dog is to be able to play with him and have a good time together. Your APBT is a sturdy fellow who loves to romp and enjoy life. Don't disappoint him. Keep your games light and fun, and remember how

Sports and Safety

Before getting started in any new sport with your dog, spend some time without him just observing the dogs and their owners who are participating. Approach competitors and find out what's involved and what your dog needs to know before you bring him out for the first time. This way, you can prepare your dog with some preliminary training. Make sure, too, that you have the right equipment before taking your dog out. Maybe you need a shade tent or an exercise pen in which to keep your dog cool and comfortable while he's waiting to compete, or perhaps he needs a tighter collar or a longer leash.

strong your APBT is. If he gets too excited and jumps on you to grab a toy, he can knock you over or hurt you. Always remind him of his manners and that nothing happens until he sits and waits. Then, let the games begin!

Teaching your APBT to retrieve is a fun way to help him channel his energy.

Resources

Associations and Organizations

Breed Clubs

American Kennel Club (AKC)
5580 Centerview Drive
Raleigh, NC 27606
Telephone: (919) 233-9767
Fax: (919) 233-3627
E-mail: info@akc.org
www.akc.org

Canadian Kennel Club (CKC)
89 Skyway Avenue, Suite 100
Etobicoke, Ontario M9W 6R4
Telephone: (416) 675-5511
Fax: (416) 675-6506
E-mail: information@ckc.ca
www.ckc.ca

Federation Cynologique Internationale (FCI)
Secretariat General de la FCI
Place Albert 1er, 13
B – 6530 Thuin
Belqique
www.fci.be

The Kennel Club
1 Clarges Street
London
W1J 8AB
Telephone: 0870 606 6750
Fax: 0207 518 1058
www.the-kennel-club.org.uk

United Kennel Club (UKC)
100 E. Kilgore Road
Kalamazoo, MI 49002-5584
Telephone: (269) 343-9020
Fax: (269) 343-7037
E-mail: pbickell@ukcdogs.com
www.ukcdogs.com

Pet Sitters

National Association of Professional Pet Sitters
15000 Commerce Parkway, Suite C
Mt. Laurel, New Jersey 08054
Telephone: (856) 439-0324
Fax: (856) 439-0525
E-mail: napps@ahint.com
www.petsitters.org

Pet Sitters International
201 East King Street
King, NC 27021-9161
Telephone: (336) 983-9222
Fax: (336) 983-5266
E-mail: info@petsit.com
www.petsit.com

Rescue Organizations and Animal Welfare Groups

American Humane Association (AHA)
63 Inverness Drive East
Englewood, CO 80112
Telephone: (303) 792-9900
Fax: 792-5333
www.americanhumane.org

American Society for the Prevention of Cruelty to Animals (ASPCA)
424 E. 92nd Street
New York, NY 10128-6804
Telephone: (212) 876-7700
www.aspca.org

Royal Society for the Prevention of Cruelty to Animals (RSPCA)
Telephone: 0870 3335 999
Fax: 0870 7530 284
www.rspca.org.uk

The Humane Society of the
United States (HSUS)
2100 L Street, NW
Washington DC 20037
Telephone: (202) 452-1100
www.hsus.org

Sports

International Agility Link (IAL)
Global Administrator: Steve Drinkwater
E-mail: yunde@powerup.au
www.agilityclick.com/~ial

North American Flyball Association
www.flyball.org
1400 West Devon Avenue #512
Chicago, IL 6066
800-318-6312

World Canine Freestyle Organization
P.O. Box 350122
Brooklyn, NY 11235-2525
Telephone: (718) 332-8336
www.worldcaninefreestyle.org

Therapy

Delta Society
875 124th Ave NE, Suite 101
Bellevue, WA 98005
Telephone: (425) 226-7357
Fax: (425) 235-1076
E-mail: info@deltasociety.org
www.deltasociety.org

Therapy Dogs Incorporated
PO Box 5868
Cheyenne, WY 82003
Telephone: (877) 843-7364
E-mail: therdog@sisna.com
www.therapydogs.com

Therapy Dogs International (TDI)
88 Bartley Road
Flanders, NJ 07836
Telephone: (973) 252-9800
Fax: (973) 252-7171
E-mail: tdi@gti.net
www.tdi-dog.org

Training

Association of Pet Dog Trainers (APDT)
150 Executive Center Drive Box 35
Greenville, SC 29615
Telephone: (800) PET-DOGS
Fax: (864) 331-0767
E-mail: information@apdt.com
www.apdt.com

**National Association of Dog Obedience
Instructors (NADOI)**
PMB 369
729 Grapevine Hwy.
Hurst, TX 76054-2085
www.nadoi.org

Veterinary and Health Resources

**American Animal Hospital Association
(AAHA)**
P.O. Box 150899
Denver, CO 80215-0899
Telephone: (303) 986-2800
Fax: (303) 986-1700
E-mail: info@aahanet.org
www.aahanet.org/index.cfm

**American Holistic Veterinary Medical
Association (AHVMA)**
2218 Old Emmorton Road
Bel Air, MD 21015
Telephone: (410) 569-0795
Fax: (410) 569-2346
E-mail: office@ahvma.org
www.ahvma.org

American Veterinary Medical Association (AVMA)
1931 North Meacham Road – Suite 100
Schaumburg, IL 60173
Telephone: (847) 925-8070
Fax: (847) 925-1329
E-mail: avmainfo@avma.org
www.avma.org

ASPCA Animal Poison Control Center
1717 South Philo Road, Suite 36
Urbana, IL 61802
Telephone: (888) 426-4435
www.aspca.org

British Veterinary Association (BVA)
7 Mansfield Street
London
W1G 9NQ
Telephone: 020 7636 6541
Fax: 020 7436 2970
E-mail: bvahq@bva.co.uk
www.bva.co.uk

Publications

Books

Anderson, Teoti. *The Super Simple Guide to Housetraining*. Neptune City: TFH Publications, 2004.

Gallagher, Cynthia. *The American Pit Bull Terrier*. Neptune City: TFH Publications, 2006.

Morgan, Diane. *Good Dogkeeping*. Neptune City: TFH Publications, 2005.

Yin, Sophia, DVM. *How to Behave So Your Dog Behaves*. Neptune City: TFH Publications, 2004.

Magazines

AKC Family Dog
American Kennel Club
260 Madison Avenue
New York, NY 10016
Telephone: (800) 490-5675
E-mail: familydog@akc.org
www.akc.org/pubs/familydog

AKC Gazette
American Kennel Club
260 Madison Avenue
New York, NY 10016
Telephone: (800) 533-7323
E-mail: gazette@akc.org
www.akc.org/pubs/gazette

Dog & Kennel
Pet Publishing, Inc.
7-L Dundas Circle
Greensboro, NC 27407
Telephone: (336) 292-4272
Fax: (336) 292-4272
E-mail: info@petpublishing.com
www.dogandkennel.com

Dog Fancy
Subscription Department
P.O. Box 53264
Boulder, CO 80322-3264
Telephone: (800) 365-4421
E-mail: barkback@dogfancy.com
www.dogfancy.com

Dogs Monthly
Ascot House
High Street, Ascot,
Berkshire SL5 7JG
United Kingdom
Telephone: 0870 730 8433
Fax: 0870 730 8431
E-mail: admin@rtc-associates.freeserve.co.uk
www.corsini.co.uk/dogsmonthly

Index

Note: Boldface numbers indicate illustrations; an italic *t* indicates a table.

109

Index

111

Index

Acknowledgements

Special thanks to Stephanie Fornino for her support and professional expertise.

About the Author

Elaine Waldorf Gewirtz is passionate about dogs and writing. In her many books and articles, she writes about canine health, care, training, and behavior. Elaine is a multiple recipient of the prestigious Maxwell Award from the Dog Writers Association of America and the ASPCA Humane Issues Award. She and her husband Steve live in Westlake Village, California, with their four-footed best friends.

Photo Credits